The Story of Becoming

Piney Flats

By Robert Sorrell

The Story of Becoming

Piney Flats

By Robert Sorrell

Laurel Fork

PUBLISHING CO. | EST. 2022

Table of Contents

Acknowledgements

I want to thank the many wonderful organizations, government agencies, and people who have graciously contributed to this book, including, in no particular order, the Piney Flats Historical Society, residents of the Piney Flats Historic District, current and former staff at the Rocky Mount State Historic Site, Rocky Mount Historical Association, Janie Torbett and the Torbett family, the National Register of Historic Places, the Tennessee Historical Commission, Tennessee Valley Authority spokeswoman Mary Ellen Miller, Tennessee Valley Authority Historian Patricia Bernard Ezzell, Tennessee State Historian Carroll Van West, former Sullivan County archivist Shelia Keen Hunt, Edgefield United Methodist Church, Piney Flats United Methodist Church, New Bethel Presbyterian Church, Bristol Historical Association, Betty Jane Hylton, Bristol Herald Courier reporter and local racing historian David McGee, Leon Johnson, Mark Carrier, and Emily Holmberg.

Introduction

The small community of Piney Flats is nestled between the waters of the Holston and Watauga rivers of Northeast Tennessee. The Holston River originates in nearby southwestern Virginia while the Watauga River starts in far western North Carolina. Both waterways cross state lines and meander through the Appalachian Mountains before meeting at a fork in Piney Flats.

Today, that fork is comprised of Boone Reservoir, a sprawling lake impoundment created by the Tennessee Valley Authority's Boone Dam and named after early American pioneer Daniel Boone.

Piney Flats sits among the rolling hills between the prongs of the fork—hence the community's early name of the Forks. Early pioneers, such as Boone, first passed through Piney Flats in the 18th century and some began settling along the banks of the rivers.

Rocky Mount State Historic Site served as the temporary capital of the Southwest Territory and is now a popular tourist site in Piney Flats. (Courtesy Rocky Mount State Historic Site)

Those early settlers bravely ventured across the Appalachian Mountains into unscathed territory, an area only touched by Cherokee native Americans and wildlife. Due to British law restricting western expansion from the 13 original colonies, the settlers moving into the Piney Flats area were doing so illegally. As a result, the early settlers were on their own without any oversight or protection.

Boone, a prolific long hunter, was one of the first white men to pass through the region. Another pioneer, William Bean Jr., joined Boone and settled in the area. He settled along the Watauga River.

Early Piney Flats later served as a temporary capital of the Southwest Territory, a U.S. territory established several years before Tennessee gained statehood. William Blount, the territorial governor, spent much of his time at Rocky Mount, where pioneer William Cobb built a log home for his family.

A Tennessee Historical Commission marker shares the story of Rocky Mount, which now serves as a state historic site.

300 yards to the southeast is the restored home of William Cobb, pioneer. First seat of government of the Southwest Territory, October 10, 1790: Governor William Blount had headquarters here until removal to Knoxville, the new Capital, in 1792. Andrew Jackson lived here six weeks while waiting for a license to practice law.

Several other pioneer families also settled along the Holston and Watauga rivers at Piney Flats, including the Masengills, DeVaults, Kings, Warrens, Hughes, and the Shells. They established farms, schools, churches, and businesses in Piney Flats.

The railroad in the 19th century brought substantial growth to Piney Flats. Trains were able to transport both goods and people to and from the community and connected it to larger cities and surrounding states. There have been several train stations in Piney Flats. The railroad's influence can especially be found today in the village, as noted in a Tennessee Historical

Passenger rail service once connected Piney Flats with towns and cities across the eastern United States. (Courtesy Piney Flats United Methodist Church)

Commission marker at the corner of U.S. Highway 11E and Piney Flats Road.

Located one mile south is historic Piney Flats Village. In 1854 construction of a railroad began in Piney Flats. Reverend Andrew Shell established the first post office and the name Piney Flats became official. In 1888 John Bunyan Wolfe founded Wolfe Bros. & Co., which manufactured household and church furniture. As the village grew, it developed its own power and telephone systems. Examples of 19th century architecture exist today throughout the village. The Piney Flats Historic District was listed in the National Register of Historic Places on November 15, 2011.

The Piney Flats Historic District was added to the National Register of Historic Places in 2011. It features several historic properties, including the Mary Hughes School, Piney Flats United Methodist Church, and multiple homes.

The historic district is filled with historic homes, the Mary Hughes School, Piney Flats United Methodist Church, an old general store, post office, and the remnants of the former Wolfe Brothers manufacturing facility. The factory once produced high quality household and church furnishings. Its pews, altars, and tables can be found at places of worship around the country. Beds, dressers, and other household items can be found in some of the old homes along Main Street in the historic district.

The Wolfe Brothers factory, which produced quality home and church furnishings for more than 100 years, closed in 2000. It was founded by local resident John Bunyan Wolfe in the 19th century. (Courtesy Piney Flats Historical Society)

Dozens of people worked at the factory, which began operations at the end of the 19th century and closed its doors in 2000. During its early years, growth at the factory required the creation of telephone and electrical services in Piney Flats, making the village one of the first in East Tennessee to have these modern conveniences.

Piney Flats, located at the center of the Tri-Cities metropolitan area, remains primarily a bedroom community in the 21st century. It consists of miles of farmland, but also modern subdivisions, mid-20th century neighborhoods, and a smattering of commercial and industrial developments.

The community remains bounded by Boone Lake, the TVA reservoir built in the mid-20th century to provide flood control and electricity. The reservoir, known for its scenery and recreation, brings thousands of people to Piney Flats every year. Several modern subdivisions and historic farms hug the shoreline.

The historic character of Piney Flats still exists, especially in the historic village, and several outlying communities, such as New Bethel and Rocky Springs, rural neighborhoods centered on historic churches. Rocky Mount State Historic Site, the home of the Cobbs and the temporary capital of the Southwest Territory, also brings many visitors to Piney Flats.

CHAPTER ONE

Early Settlement

The history of Piney Flats begins in the mid-18th century, long before Tennessee gained statehood and America was still just a young British colony. This vast region was quite desolate when pioneers first ventured west from the 13 original colonies that bordered the Atlantic Ocean. At the time, the Proclamation of 1763 made it illegal for pioneers to cross the mountains into present-day Tennessee, so those that did had to fend for themselves. The British monarch approved the proclamation in order to keep colonists from moving to French-owned lands west of the mountains.

Before white pioneers explored the area, the Cherokee called the region home, including in Piney Flats. Through various treaties, the Cherokee relinquished their lands in Northeast Tennessee.

Frontiersman Daniel Boone and dog are pictured here in the American wilderness. Boone visited Northeast Tennessee in the 18th century. (Courtesy National Archives)

Legendary early American frontiersman Daniel Boone may be one of the first to have traveled into Piney Flats. He first ventured west of the Appalachian Mountains between 1769 and 1775. Boone blazed trails across large swaths of land from North Carolina to Missouri. He was one of the most notable "long hunters" of the era, a term given to a number of men accustomed to spending long continuous periods of time hunting in the regions west of the Appalachian Mountains. Many, like Boone, began their journeys in the 13 colonies, particularly North Carolina and Virginia, and ventured west over the mountains.

The long hunters would travel alone for weeks, if not months, at a time, exploring the wilds, encountering dangerous animals, quiet, lonely landscapes, and Native Americans. The explorers often followed major waterways through the desolate regions.

It is not known when Boone, born in 1734, made his first journey into what is now northeastern Tennessee and passed through or near Piney Flats. At some point in 1760, Boone is believed to have hidden under a waterfall near the Watauga River -- which he was following -- to hide from raiding Native Americans, according to the Tennessee Historical Commission.

Later, local residents in the Boone's Creek community discovered a beech tree with the phrase "D. Boon cilled a bar on tree in the year 1760" etched into the wood. Boone was known to kill bears on his adventures and marked trees along the way.

The tree became a popular tourist destination in the late 1800s and early 1900s. But local newspapers reported about the tree's ultimate destruction in June of 1916 when a strong thunderstorm swept through the area, splitting the famed tree in half.

"A number of people have visited it since that time," The Post of Big Stone Gap, Virginia, reported at the time. "Those who have seen it state that it can never be preserved unless it is taken and preserved by some society or organization."

It remained in the forest until Lafayette Isley, the property owner, sold it to Z.A. Robertson, who had the trunk sawed into slabs and the limbs into shorter length in order to make souvenirs, according to a report in the Johnson City Press. Most of the wood was stored by Robertson until the John Sevier chapter of the Daughters of the American Revolution bought what was left.

A portion of the fallen Boone tree was sent to the Wolfe Brothers Factory in Piney Flats, where the wood was transformed into gavels, according to the Piney Flats Historical Society. Current local Piney Flats resident John Starnes, a Wolfe family descendent, owns one of the gavels. Others have been given to former Tennessee Governor Lamar Alexander, First Lady Eleanor Roosevelt, and Vice President Richard Nixon, the Johnson City Press reported. The Friends of the Washington County, Tennessee Archives reports that about 500 gavels were produced. Television star Fess Parker, who portrayed Boone in a popular 1960s television show, also received several items from the tree, including a gavel. E.W. Hughes, a Wolfe

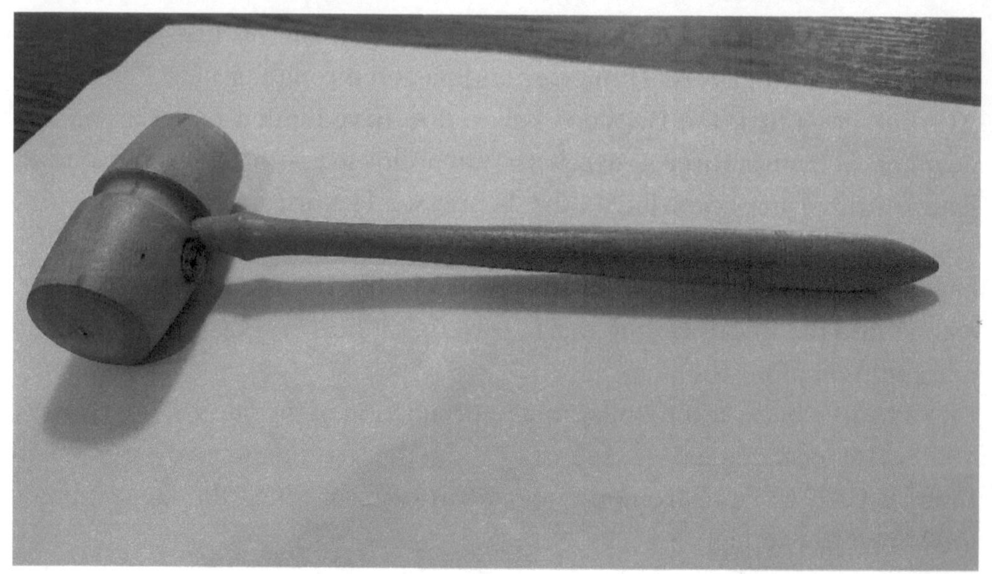

Several wood mallets or gavels were produced at the Wolfe Brothers factory in Piney Flats after it received remnants of the famous tree pioneer Daniel Boone signed in the 1700s. A Piney Flats resident owns the item pictured above. (Photo by author)

Brothers employee, wrote a letter to Tennessee historian Samuel Heiskell about the gavels, according to history columnist Bob Cox. Hughes first notified Heiskell that his factory had four fabricated gavels ready to send him.

Boone likely traveled through northeast Tennessee on multiple occasions. In 1775, Richard Henderson, a prominent North Carolina judge, hired Boone to travel to Cherokee communities across the region, inviting them to a meeting along the Watauga River in present-day Elizabethton, Tennessee. There, during what was known as the Transylvania Purchase, the parties signed the Treaty of Sycamore Shoals, allowing Henderson to purchase large amounts of land in Kentucky and Tennessee. Henderson then hired Boone to blaze what eventually became known as the Wilderness Trail, which stretched from northeast Tennessee to central Kentucky. In the early 20th century, several markers were placed along Boone's route, including a monument along Austin Springs Road near Piney Flats.

Several other long hunters and explorers often joined Boone's expeditions, including pioneer William Bean Jr., who became known as the first permanent white settler in Tennessee. Bean, from Virginia, built a cabin in 1769 on the south side of the Watauga River at Boone's Creek in present day Washington County. Russell Bean, the first child of permanent Tennessee settlers, was born at the cabin, a Tennessee Historical Commission marker states.

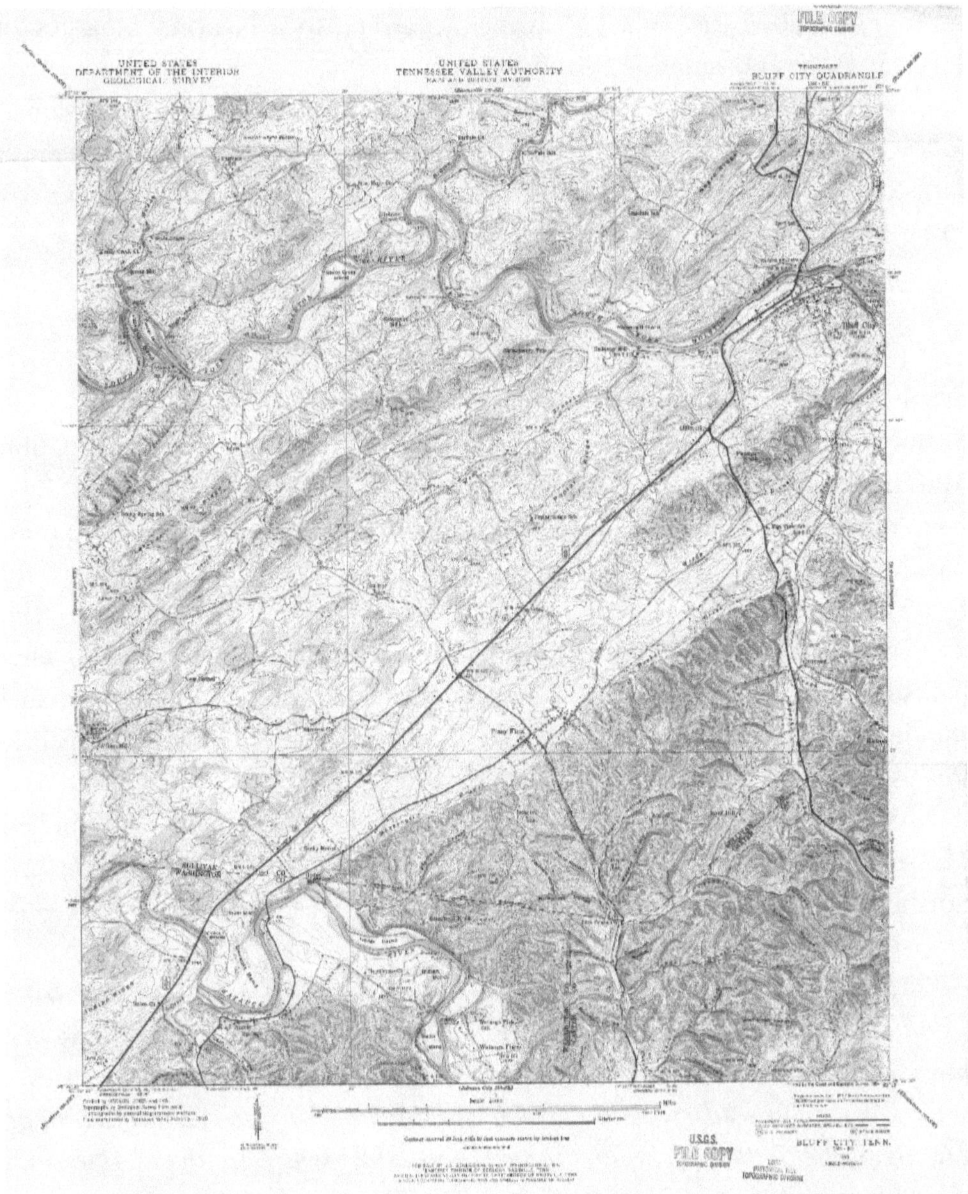

Topographic map from the U.S. Geological Survey of the Holston and Watauga rivers.

One of Bean's brothers, John Bean, also settled along the southern banks of the Watauga River. He built a cabin, which reportedly was later dismantled and floated across the river to Piney Flats. The historic Bean cabin was reconstructed at the Valentine DeVault Farm, which is located in Piney Flats along the Watauga River, according to a National Register of Historic Places nomination form.

Dozens of other families—from Virginia, Maryland, and Pennsylvania--followed the Beans to Tennessee, and they also settled along the Watauga, Holston, and Nolichucky rivers. Many of those families settled in present-day Piney Flats.

Masengill and DeVault settlements

John Bean — whose cabin was transported across the Watauga River — eventually sold his land to another early Piney Flats pioneer, Henry Masengill Sr., who settled in the region from Virginia in 1769 with his wife Mary Cobb Masengill, according to a National Register of Historic Places form. The couple originally built a three-story log structure, which is now gone, on their farm, located today at the intersection of U.S. Highway 11E and Edgefield Road in Piney Flats.

In the 1770s, the couple also constructed another small one and one-half story log building, which is believed to have housed slaves, and remains standing on the property, according to the National Register of Historic Places, which recognized the property in 1985.

Without any religious facilities in the region, Masengill--also spelled Massengill and Massengale--established a house of worship along the northern banks of the Watauga River.

"In April 1777, Rev. Charles Cummings, a Presbyterian minister from Wolf Hills Settlement [in southwest Virginia] came to Watauga and preached three days," Henry Masengill wrote. "We hailed his coming among us with great joy, for our souls were hungering and thirsting for spiritual nourishment. He urged the Settlers to build a house of worship, which we decided to do. I was to furnish logs, boards and all timbers needed to build a large house, with a section of benches in the back side for the Massengill and Cobb negroes

numbering at this time 151 souls. So these slaves can come out and be refreshed in body and soul. This house was completed by July 1777, and known as the Massengill House of Worship. Rev. Cummings and Mulkey preached several times to the settlers."

While Masengill was away from the settlement in 1779, "Tories came, abused my family, destroyed my property, burnt the Massengill House of Worship to the ground."

Masengill also served as a member of the Watauga Association, a semi-autonomous government comprised in 1772 by the settlers of the Watauga, Holston, and Nolichucky river valleys. The frontier government ended upon American independence in 1776 and the establishment of the states of North Carolina (1789) and Tennessee (1796).

The Pioneer Monument is located today at Winged Deer Park in Johnson City, Tennessee. It was first erected at the direction of Dr. Samuel Evans Masengill, Henry Masengill's great-great grandson. It was previously located at the intersection of two highes that lead to Bristol and Kingsport. (Courtesy Betty Jane Hylton)

The Pioneer Monument in Johnson City recognizes Masengill's importance in the region's history. It was first erected in north Johnson City at the direction of Dr. Samuel Evans Masengill, Henry's great-great grandson, at the intersection of two highways leading to Bristol and Kingsport. The monument was moved in 1990 to Winged Deer Park.

"Erected to the memory of Henry Massengill and his pioneer family

Came from North Carolina to the Watauga Settlement in 1769. His plantation near the mouth of Boone's Creek adjoined William Bean's, who was the first permanent white settler west of the Alleghany Mountains.

In 1775 was appointed to an office in the Watauga Association which adopted the first written constitution for the government of American-born freemen.

Built the Massengill house of worship, 1777, served two years as sheriff of Washington District. In 1778 was chairman of the Committee of Safety.

Served on the staff of Captain William Edmiston in General's Shelby's expedition against the Chicamagua Indians in 1779.

Furnished three sons to the Revolutionary Army."

The DeVault family settled in the Piney Flats area in 1800 and their mark can be found in two historic homes near U.S. Highway 11E, not far from the Watauga River. Brothers Frederick and Valentine DeVault--also spelled Devault and Dewald--inherited land from their parents, Henry and Mary Catherine DeVault, according to National Register of Historic Places forms regarding their homes. Henry DeVault, also named Heinrich and Henri in various records, who immigrated from the French-German border and arrived in America in 1766, served in the Revolutionary War at Valley Forge in Pennsylvania. With money from his service in the war, DeVault traveled at least twice to Tennessee to purchase land. He willed the land holdings to four of his 11 children, including Valentine, Frederick, Gabriel, and Henry, the forms state.

His son Gabriel DeVault first settled along the Watauga River at Piney Flats in an area called DeVault Ford, where pioneers could cross the river. Beginning in 1798, according to Washington County court records, Gabriel

20

The stately Valentine DeVault home is located along Boone Lake in Piney Flats. The home was added to the National Register of Historic Places in 1977. Built before the Civil War, it is one of Tennessee's oldest brick residences. (Photo by author)

is believed to have operated a ferry across the river to the Bean plantation. He later went with his brother Henry to another section of Piney Flats, just south of the Holston River in the Cross settlement.

Valentine and Frederick divided the land they inherited in Sullivan and Washington counties. Valentine obtained the land along the Watauga River at Piney Flats and Frederick settled in the community of Leesburg in Washington County, about 20 miles from present-day downtown Johnson City.

In 1837, Valentine DeVault purchased additional land from Masengill, who owned the property adjacent to the DeVault property, a National Register of Historic Places form states.

DeVault built a large Federal-style house on his property, which was located along the Watauga River. The beautiful brick structure is about two miles from the Masengill homestead. Today, it faces northeast at the end of Degrasse Lane, just east of U.S. Highway 11E.

The home's original portion consisted of a two-story rectangular shape, seven-bay principal mass, one room deep with an attached wing extending out from the center of the rear wall, according to the form. Like other brick homes at the time, the home was constructed of brick made on the property. The exterior is said to feature carved detailed windows which were brought to the site from Virginia, the form states. At the time of the National Register nomination, the inside floors and woodwork were original.

The home was built between 1835 and 1842, according to the nomination form. Some sources say the house was built by John Lyles in 1842; other sources relate it was constructed in 1835 by a Mr. Hall who had a crew of slave laborers.

The rear wing was first enlarged in 1890. In recent years, the home has been expanded and large columns have been added to the street-facing façade.

The Valentine DeVault House features some similar architectural details as the DeVault Tavern, which was built in 1820 by Fredrick DeVault in Leesburg.

The Bean cabin, which was reconstructed on the DeVault property from across the river, no longer exists. The DeVault property is now bordered to the south by Boone Lake, which was created by the impoundment of the Watauga River in the mid-20th century, and the nearby DeVault Bridge carries U.S. Highway 11E across the lake. Several modern luxury homes line Degrasse Lane, including a neighboring unique multi-million-dollar castle built in the late 1990s by automobile dealer Steven Grindstaff.

Henry Masengill, who owned the property adjacent to the DeVaults, had six children. One of the children, Henry "Hal" Masengill Jr., became a large landowner, as evident in Washington County grants and deeds, according to family records compiled by Samuel E. Masengil. In a family history book, Masengill Jr. is described as a "small man of positive character, black eyes, heavy eye-brows, high tempered, but generous and just." He also married three times, including to his first wife Penelope Cobb, daughter of another early Piney Flats pioneer, William Cobb, who lived nearby at Rocky Mount.

Masengill Jr.'s name can be found on several court records from Washington and Sullivan counties, including a 1793 lawsuit regarding a mare. In the suit, Masengill complains of John Tipton about Tipton's failure to appear with his mare at a racetrack and "to keep her in sweats and running order or condition." Both had agreed to this, and Tipton failed to bring his mare, according to court records. It states that Masengill fulfilled his promise and said Tipton had "contriving and fraudulently intending craftily and subtilely to deceive the said Henry in this respect and that he [Henry] is injured and hath damage of Five Hundred pounds. Therefore, he brings this suit and there are pledges to prosecution."

Rocky Mount's staff believes the horse track was located in Johnson City, near the present-day mall. Tipton resided on the south side of Johnson City, which is now home to the Tipton-Haynes Historic Site.

Several early Washington and Sullivan county families, including the Masengills of Piney Flats, were slaveowners. In 1820, Masengill Jr. sold slaves to his grandson, according to the Rocky Mount archives. A court document states: "Full compensation for my negro boy Dick. Likewise, Annas, his wife, and their children named Moses, Jenny and Matildah, which negroes I warrant and forever defend from the lawful claim or claims of any person or persons whatsoever the wench and children to be his property from this present date and the feller is his property at my death."

In 1825, Masengill Jr. sold 385 acres of land to the DeVault family, according to records. The tract of land was comprised of the original log structures at U.S. Highway 11E and Edgefield Road in Piney Flats.

The DeVault-Masengill Home is located along U.S. Highway 11E in Piney Flats. It features an old log cabin and a larger brick residence. The property was added to the National Register of Historic Places in 1984, when these two photographs were taken. (Courtesy Tennessee Historical Commission)

By 1842, Valentine DeVault's son, Isaac DeVault, resided in the old Masengill log house and directed property, the two-story structure, which still stands in Piney Flats, is known as the DeVault-Masengill House. The main section is three-bays wide and one-room deep. A two-story ell extends from the northwest corner of the house. There are also four chimneys projecting from the home.

Inside, the home features exquisite details throughout, including elaborate ceiling medallions and a paneled staircase. Many of the floors are original, including the handmade nails used during the time of construction. Walnut, cherry, and other woods can be found throughout the home.

In the library, the walnut bookcases and fireplace frontal, mantel and crown molding came from trees cut from the farm. There are also two unique medallions crafted into the ceiling near the main entrance. Local realtor Loretta Trayer said some Italian plasterers came through the area and the Masengills hired them to create the medallions.

The slave cabin, which still stands about 30 feet from the brick house, has a gable roof covered with cedar shakes, and a porch spanning the south front facade. A large limestone chimney is on the western side of the building.

The DeVault family owned the home until 1906 when the Wexler family purchased the property. The Masengill family, who had established the farm in the 18th century, regained possession of the property in 1938. Sally Masengill restored the home in 1984 with the help of architect Frank McCaul and contractor Harold Welch.

Masengill descendants began to sell portions of the property in the 21st century. But before its sale, the property was considered the oldest recognized family farm in the state, according to the Tennessee Century Farms program.

The Rocky Mount State Historic Site is located in Piney Flats, just outside of Johnson City, along U.S. Highway 11E. (Courtesy Rocky Mount State Historic Site)

Rocky Mount State Historic Site

The Rocky Mount State Historic Site was first established in the late 18th century along present-day U.S. Highway 11E in Piney Flats. It's located near the old Masengill farm. The legendary site, founded by pioneer William Cobb, served temporarily as the capital of the Southwest Territory, according to Tennessee-sanctioned studies.

William Cobb is believed to have come to the Watauga River settlement in the 1760s, long before Tennessee became a state in 1796. He served as a justice of the peace when the North Carolina legislature created Washington County, which then covered Sullivan and Washington counties in Tennessee. He also served as a commissioner to lay out the town of Jonesborough, Tennessee's first town, which is located less than 15 miles away from Rocky Mount.

Cobb first built a home in the area in about 1770. His home served as a beacon light in the early pioneer settlement near the Watauga River, a

26

This vintage image of the Masengill family of Piney Flats is from 1897. They are pictured at Rocky Mount. (Courtesy Rocky Mount State Historic Site)

National Register of Historic Places document states. Other early pioneers, including Boone (the frontiersman), John Sevier (who became Tennessee's first governor), William Campbell, Richard Henderson, and Isaac Shelby spent time at Rocky Mount. Andrew Jackson, who later became president in 1829, stayed at Rocky Mount for a few weeks as he waited to obtain his license to practice law in Jonesborough. Jackson was a relative of Cobb's wife, Barsheba.

A group of men on their way to the Battle of King's Mountain—a turning point in the Revolutionary War—also stopped by Rocky Mount in the fall of 1780. According to tradition, Cobb outfitted more than 900 men with bacon, horses, bullets, and slave labor. It is thought that this group of men camped here on Sept. 24, 1780. Cobb and four of his sons, Arthur, Jerry, Pharoh, and William Jr., joined the Overmountain Men, named so for crossing the Appalachian Mountains to reach Kings Mountain in South Carolina.

The men likely stopped at Rocky Mount on their way to nearby Sycamore Shoals at present-day Elizabethton, which served as a mustering point for the men of Tennessee and Virginia. The men were responding to

British Major Patrick Ferguson, who issued a challenge to the Appalachian-region leaders to lay down their arms or he would "lay waste to their country with fire and sword."

After defeating the British army at Kings Mountain—in what Thomas Jefferson later said was "the turn of the tide of success which terminated the Revolutionary War with the seal of our independence"—the Overmountain Men returned to Tennessee, many again stopping at Rocky Mount. An Overmountain Victory Trail marker can now be found at the Rocky Mount State Historic Site.

Almost 20 years later when North Carolina ceded its western lands to the United States and the area south of the Ohio River was created, President George Washington appointed William Blount as Southwest Territory governor. Blount visited Washington's Mount Vernon in September 1790, when he was sworn in as governor. Then, in October 1790, Blount set up a temporary capital at Rocky Mount and began to organize a government.

Blount carried on territorial business at Rocky Mount from 1790 until 1792, when the capital moved to Knoxville. The governor worked to forge peace between the distinctive Native American tribes and settlers, train a professional state militia, and, among a host of other tasks, oversee the

28

The Cobb house
has been
meticulously
restored and
remodeled over
the years at Rocky
Mount State
Historic Site.
(Courtesy Rocky
Mount State
Historic Site)

enumeration of the territory's population, according to the U.S. Census Bureau.

According to Blount's 1790-91 census return, the Southwest Territory had a population of 35,691, which was less than the threshold of 60,000 people required for a territory to become a state.

On Oct. 20, 1790, Blount wrote: "At William Cobb's, Washington County ... On the 11th instant, I arrived in this county, and was received with every mark of attention and gladness that I could have wished. I am very well accommodated with a Room with Glass Windows, Fireplace, etc., etc., at this place."

Sometime after 1792, the Cobb family moved from Rocky Mount, but Masengill Jr., who had married Cobb's daughter Penelope, took possession of the property, named for its rocky outcropping. The house remained in the Masengill family for four generations, and even served at one time as a post office. After 1900, tenants occupied the house for a while until the state of Tennessee purchased it in 1959.

The home standing at Rocky Mount today was built in the 1820s, likely by the Masengill family, according to the Tennessee Historical Commission and an early 21st century study of the rings of the structure's logs.

Based on a 2007 historical archaeology report, Rocky Mount is the site of the early Southwest Territory capital, but its buildings belong to a later date, Tennessee State Historian Carroll Van West said.

The current main house at Rocky Mount is a nine-room, two-story house constructed of white oak logs cut from the surrounding area, a National Register of Historic Places document states. There was a large, hipped chimney of brick at the left and in the ell at the back, it states.

Very few changes were made to the home until the late 19th century, when the logs were covered with weatherboarding and the outside kitchen was moved to the inside. A new dining room was added to the north side of the kitchen and the dogtrot became a bedroom, the document states.

Following the state's purchase in the 20th century, the earlier renovations were removed, and the house was converted back to its original shape. The weatherboarding was removed, and cedar shake shingles were placed on the roof, instead of white oak shingles which it originally had.

After the state purchased the property, crews restored Rocky Mount under the direction of Pauline Massengill DeFriece, a descendant of the original settlers. DeFriece, a prominent Bristol resident and property owner's cousin, believed that the building should be preserved by the state and be opened to the public as a showplace to the memory of the early settlers of the region.

DeFriece set in motion the chain of events that led to the purchase of Rocky Mount by the state of Tennessee, according to the Rocky Mount Historical Association, which she also helped establish.

The original dedication of the Rocky Mount State Historic Site was held on Oct. 29, 1961, and was witnessed by more than 5,000 people, according to the Bristol Herald Courier.

"We had expected only 300 or 400," DeFriece told the newspaper. April 1, 1962, marked the opening of the new Rocky Mount Museum and the old log house. DeFriece was on hand to greet visitors and said at the time she hoped all children would be able to tour the museum and houses, "because they depict the life of their ancestors."

DeFriece said one of her favorite portraits in the museum, which now has numerous family and pioneer artifacts, has a "romance" behind it. The painting is of Susan Massengill Porter.

The romance relates to how Susan Massengill met her husband, Alexander James Porter, who later became a Nashville financier. Porter was from Delaware and migrated to the west, according to the newspaper.

"Coming into this territory, he became ill and fell from a horse in front of Susan Massengill's home," DeFriece said. "When he recovered about seven weeks later, Porter married Susan and they moved to Nashville."

In addition to the museum, several outbuildings have been added to the property which are intended to depict life in the 18th century.

A home for a caretaker was built in 1975, and in 1979, the visitor center, originally built for the opening, was expanded to include a museum gift shop.

In 1990, a 175-seat auditorium with video output, library, and four classrooms were added to the property, according to the site.

The historic site was also expanded to include a kitchen, springhouse, and slave cabin, barn, orchard, and gardens to enhance the living history atmosphere of the Cobb farm.

Patrick McIntyre Jr., of the state Historical Commission, which still owns the property, said, "Millions of dollars have gone into the preservation of this property over the past 60 years, and hundreds of thousands of visitors have gone there to learn the story of the old Southwest Territorial capitol. And Rocky Mount State Historic Site will continue to be where this important story is shared with visitors, along with interpreting life on the frontier."

The Rocky Mount Historical Association manages the site and tours are provided by costumed living history reenactors. It also hosts events throughout the year, including sheep shearing and an old-fashioned baseball game. The sheep, a popular attraction at Rocky Mount, are raised on the property.

CHAPTER TWO

The Forks

Following in the footsteps of the early pioneers, such as the Beans, Masengills, Cobbs, and DeVaults, who settled near the banks of the Watauga River, other settlers of European descent also began to settle in Piney Flats. In its infancy, Piney Flats was simply known as the Forks because of the fork created by the convergence of the Watauga and Holston rivers at present-day Boone Lake.

Occasionally, many of the settlers at the Forks would meet at a place they called the "pine flats." This place was so named due to the presence of native pine trees on land that sloped gradually toward the Watauga River.

The settlers often gathered to organize hunts to go after wolves that were a menace to local livestock, a common issue in early American history. The pioneers had cattle, sheep, pigs, and horses on their properties, which attracted wolves. With little protection, livestock often died.

In order to save their animals, early Piney Flats residents began baiting and hunting the wolves, eradicating them from the region. Ultimately, wolves became extinct in the Appalachian Mountains, even though they were a native species.

Early Sullivan County historian Oliver Taylor wrote about the different types of hunters in the Holston region, including those that hunted for wolves. Taylor described both transient and resident hunters. Transient hunters, Taylor said, would travel for long distances, hunt for animals, and then return home. Resident hunters would simply settle in the area and hunt. Then, there were "round-up" and "fire" hunters. These two kinds of hunters often worked in organized bands and protected their homes against "the ravages of the wild beasts than for sport or for sustenance," Taylor wrote.

The "round-up" hunts were especially directed against wolves, such as those in Piney Flats. Sometimes more than one hundred men would engage in the round-up. They would encircle a large boundary of land and drive the animals toward the center, gradually closing in upon them and giving but little chance of escape, Taylor wrote.

"For a long time that section was infested with packs of vicious and destructive wolves – which were made more bold by the veneration of the Indians for them – and the neighborhood hunters, agreeing upon a 'meet,' would name 'the flats,'" Taylor wrote.

Later, as the wolf population waned, wolf hunting was replaced with fox hunting, but the same meeting place was used, and the young community's name evolved into Piney Flats.

A few families moved into "the flats," including the Shells, who were primarily responsible for the early development of the Piney Flats community.

In 1782, 400 acres of land south of the Holston River was granted to Arnold Shell for a "sum of fifty shillings for every hundred acres," according to a land grant from the state of North Carolina, which was still in control of the land at the time. Also in 1782, Edward and Elizabeth King were issued a land grant of 640 acres in Piney Flats.

Shell's son Andrew Shell was born in 1797 on the banks of the Holston River, just north of Bluff City. He married Winifred Boy Shell and the couple moved to Indiana and had two children, one of whom died. Several years later, the couple returned to Tennessee and settled in Piney Flats.

By the 1840s, Shell, a Methodist reverend, became a circuit-riding preacher. According to the 1850 census in Sullivan County, Reverend Shell owned 3,000 acres of land, including a significant amount of land on Piney Flats. In 1873, he donated an acre of land on a pine knoll in Piney Flats on which a union church was built.

Construction of Shell's Chapel, the church came to be known, was accomplished by men of four different Christian denominations: Baptist, Presbyterian, Methodist Episcopal, and Methodist Episcopal Church South. All four groups used the white frame weatherboard structure with a traditional belfry. By the time of the church's construction, Reverend Shell had retired from riding the circuit. However, he would occasionally preach a short sermon at the church. The Reverend Mr. Lucas, an Englishman, was the first pastor of the church.

Named after Shell, the community in the 19th century was known as Shell's Crossroads or Shell's Crossings until a railroad and post office came to town.

When the East Tennessee and Virginia Railroad was being constructed in the area, Shell applied for a post office with the idea of accommodating the laborers. His request was granted, and as a result Shell became the first postmaster. In 1855, the name "Piney Flats" became official. The first post office was located in Shell's home, which was located in a wooded hollow south of the present-day village. His receipts from 1855 through 1860 totaled $20.01. Shell served as postmaster for five years, a job that paid him a total of $12.

Reverend Shell died in April 1880. He was buried under an oak tree at the top of a hill on his farm. Legend has it that Shell tended and cared for the oak tree from the time when it was very young. He chose the shade of the tree as the place at which he would be laid to rest. As years went by, members of his family were also buried there, as well as his friends. Eventually, others who never knew Shell were buried there. Today, it's known as Shell's Cemetery and is located adjacent to present day- Piney Flats United

Methodist Church. A small committee now manages the cemetery, which is still in use.

The Railroad Comes to Piney Flats

The railroad has always played a major role in Piney Flats' history. It brought growth and prosperity from the moment it came to town—connecting the village and surrounding areas to larger cities across the country. Trains have often given local residents a chance to find work, bring in goods and services, and travel. It's also given local industries the opportunity to transport products.

Before 1850, to get goods and services that were not available in Piney Flats, local residents traveled to nearby communities, such as Bristol and Johnson City, by horseback or wagon. They followed old Native American trails and paths that pioneers once used. Industrious Piney Flats residents also established ferries to carry passengers across the Holston and Watauga rivers. It would take all day, or even overnight, to travel back and forth between Piney Flats and nearby towns.

As the year 1850 began, there were no railroad tracks in service in Tennessee. There was, however, a plan for connecting the major cities of the state with one another and with the remainder of the country. As the 1850s progressed, rail construction took place, eventually connecting Memphis with Nashville and Nashville with Chattanooga. Chattanooga had a rail connection to the east coast by way of the Western and Atlantic Railroad. Knoxville was to be brought into the network through construction of the East Tennessee and Georgia Railroad, which would link with the Western and Atlantic in Dalton, Georgia. The final piece of the rail project would connect Knoxville with railroads in Virginia, passing through places such as Johnson City, Bristol, and Piney Flats.

While the Tennessee railroads were being built, tracks were being laid southwest from Lynchburg, Virginia, to the Tennessee/Virginia state line at Bristol. The Virginia and Tennessee Railroad would end at the state line because, at the time, most railroads were allowed to operate in only one state and had to be funded by state bonds. Bristol, Tennessee, which is located about 20 miles from Piney Flats, owes its existence and location to the fact that Joseph R. Anderson, the town's founder,

purchased property. He planned and surveyed the town to be located where the Virginia and Tennessee Railroad would intersect the state line.

With the Virginia and Tennessee joining the East Tennessee and Virginia at Bristol, a chain of railroads would form a continuous link from Memphis to the major cities of Virginia and the northeast U.S.

The prospect of northeastern Tennessee being included in the railroad network meant a lot to the region's economic outlook.

Since the introduction of steamboats on America's major waterways, such as the Mississippi, Missouri, and Ohio rivers, upper east Tennessee had become isolated. Flatboats were able to travel downstream on the Holston River transporting raw materials to cities along the Mississippi River and ultimately the international port at the Gulf of Mexico in New Orleans. Unlike steamboats, flatboats had no mechanical power and could not make the return trip to northeast Tennessee. The Holston and Watauga rivers were not suitable for steamboats, as they were not navigable.

A flatboat has a flat bottom and are typically rectangular so they could transport freight. Flatboats were often used to transport goods in shallow waters. They were almost always used one way and would be dismantled when they reached their destination.

A railroad through the region would completely change the situation and connect places like Piney Flats with the rest of the country.

A group of delegates met in Greeneville, Tennessee, on July 15, 1847, to discuss the possibility of making improvements to the Holston River that would make it navigable for steamboats, according to newspapers and a written history of Piney Flats that was made for the National Register of Historic Places. During the course of the meeting, there was some discussion to fund a railroad. The rivers never were made navigable, but the meeting provided the impetus for construction of the railroad. The Tennessee legislature passed an act which incorporated the East Tennessee and Virginia on January 21, 1849, and the company was officially organized on November 21.

One of the first decisions to be made was to determine the route. Three proposed routes were surveyed, and construction costs were estimated for each one. Of the routes, the southernmost was determined to be two miles longer than the other two but would cost less by about a quarter million dollars. The southern route was better in terms of grades and curves. The most persuasive factor in deciding among the proposals was the fact that the southern route would go through an area that, at the time, had more businesses that would be more likely to use the railroad.

That decision was important to the establishment and growth of Piney Flats. The route chosen for the railroad would pass through the area where early settlers had met to organize wolf hunts.

Construction contracts were executed in 1852 and work began at both ends of the route. At the eastern end, construction of the first 20 miles of track, from the Virginia border to the Watauga River, began in October, according to the written history. Masonry work on the bridge spanning the Holston River was nearly complete by May 1853. Upon completion of the bridge, the same construction crew was to immediately begin building the bridge over the Watauga River. There is no record as to when construction at the Watauga River began. Evidence indicates that much of the grading was accomplished in 1853 and 1854, the written history states.

East Tennessee and Virginia Railroad construction was halted in 1855 for several reasons, the written history states. The price of rail-related goods soared because, at the time, railroads were being constructed all over the world and demand had risen. Also, the United States experienced a depression a few years before the panic of 1857 and the state's bonds, which provided funding for the railroad, could not be sold. It was also noted that construction on the Virginia and Tennessee had not progressed as much as planned.

The weather also averted construction efforts. No work took place from the first snow until the arrival of spring.

By the end of 1856, the Virginia and Tennessee had completed its tracks to Bristol and 10 miles of track had been laid at the east end of the East Tennessee and Virginia.

Passenger rail service once provided residents in Piney Flats a way to travel across the country. The local train route went from Bristol to Knoxville, and included stops in Johnson City, Greeneville, and other communities across East Tennessee. Passenger service eventually stopped operating in Piney Flats and the depot was no longer needed. It was eventually demolished and replaced by a small building. (Courtesy Piney Flats Historical Society)

The last rail was laid by the president of the railroad on May 14, 1858, and the first through-train service began on May 17. From that date, Piney Flats had a place on the network of rails that stretched from the east coast to the Mississippi River. The railroad is still in use today and is part of the Norfolk Southern Railroad.

Piney Flats' first train depot was constructed about 1858, according to newspaper reports. Railroad maps from the period label the place as "Shell's Station." The depot was then replaced in 1900 by a more permanent structure which was built across the tracks from the original location.

The Southern Railway Company had decided to erect a new depot at Piney Flats in 1899, according to an article in the Knoxville Sentinel. One by one, the old "shacks" along the railroad were disappearing and new spacious buildings were taking their places.

"That village has been in need of a larger station house for some time," the newspaper reported.

The Southern Railway later discontinued its agency at Piney Flats on March 16, 1938, and no passenger or express service was provided.

In July 1957, the Southern Railway Company was then given permission by the Tennessee Public Service Commission to tear down the 1900 depot building. The authority was given after a hearing in Knoxville before Commissioner Hammond Fowler. There was no protest to the petition filed by the railway company, according to an article in the Sullivan County News.

A suitable waiting shed was ordered to be built when the depot structure was removed. The depot was demolished in 1958.

The automobile and road development made passenger service in Piney Flats and elsewhere in East Tennessee obsolete. Freight trains continue to transport a variety of goods through Piney Flats in the 21st century. Several trains pass through the community every day.

CHAPTER THREE

American Civil War

Like much of the country, Northeast Tennessee was deeply divided during the American Civil War, which lasted for four years between 1861 and 1865. However, Confederate sentiment may have been stronger in Sullivan County—where Piney Flats is located—than any other portion of the region. The county voted for Tennessee to secede from the Union in special elections in 1861, according to the book Families and History of Sullivan County, Tennessee.

Sullivan County's close proximity to Virginia, the fact that it had the highest cotton and tobacco production in Northeast Tennessee, the region's highest slave population, and its overwhelming support for the 1860 Democratic Party candidate demonstrates Sullivan County's close connection with the south, according to the report, Internal Dissent: East Tennessee's Civil War, 1849-1865, which was written by East Tennessee State University graduate Meredith Anne Grant.

Grant said there was constant internal fighting in the region and East Tennesseans were forced to cope daily with violence and constant scavenging from both the Union and Confederate forces. She said the region was home to constant guerilla warfare that turned neighbors against one another and brothers and against brothers.

If one were to take a walk through any historic cemetery in Piney Flats today, one is like to discover graves of soldiers that fought on either side of the battle. Shell Cemetery and New Bethel Cemetery both feature Union and Confederate graves.

While the railroad brought progress to Piney Flats, Grant said it also led the region to become increasingly connected to the south, both financially and ideologically. As a result, the railroad became vitally important for both sides during the conflict.

Confederate senator Landon Carter Haynes of Tennessee wrote to Confederate President Jefferson Davis that "I am looking every moment also to hear that the bridges have been burned and the East Tennessee and Virginia Railroad torn up. Nothing can save it but a sufficient guard. The Confederate States have no marshal in East, Middle, or West Tennessee to assist in keeping the peace. Ought they not be appointed?"

Haynes asked Confederate Secretary of War LeRoy Walker for Confederate troops to come to Tennessee to discourage Union support. Walker agreed.

In late 1862, Union supporters in northeast Tennessee devised a plan to burn bridges along the railroad to stop Confederate supplies. Under the direction of William Carter, the men set out on Nov. 8, 1862, to attack nine bridges.

The men first targeted and burned the Chickamauga Creek and Hiwassee bridges in southeast Tennessee. Both were poorly guarded. The Lick Creek and Union bridges in Greene County were also burned. However, bridges at Bridgeport, Loudon, and Watauga were heavily guarded by Confederate soldiers and efforts were abandoned.

Then, on December 30, 1862, after Christmas and before the New Year, Samuel P. Carter of Elizabethton and a group of Union soldiers returned to the bridges at the Watauga and Holston rivers. The men were able to defeat

Confederate soldiers and burned the bridges in events known as Carter's Raid.

More than a year later, Union soldiers passed through Piney Flats again while enroute to Blountville, where they battled Confederate troops.

On Sept. 22, 1963, Union Col. John W. Foster engaged Confederate Col. James E. Carter. Foster attacked at noon and in the four-hour battle shelled the town, compelling Confederates to withdraw.

A Battle of Blountville historic marker states: "After delaying the Union advance for more than four hours, Carter withdrew toward Zollicoffer, now known as Bluff City. During the battle, artillery shells set fire to the courthouse and much of the town burned. Skirmishing continued until news of the bloody battle at Chickamauga reached General Ambrose Burnside, and Union General Henry Wager Halleck ordered a retreat toward Knoxville."

At the time of the battle, Confederate soldiers had occupied Blountville while Federal forces held the Watauga River.

Troops often passed through the farms of Piney Flats enroute to battles and skirmishes, such as those at the river bridges and Blountville.

Post-War Reimbursement

After the war, the U.S. Congress created the Southern Claims Commission, which was tasked to receive, examine, and consider claims submitted by southern Unionist citizens. Claimants sought compensation for supplies that had been confiscated by or furnished to the U.S. Army during the war.

The commission would certify that the citizens were loyal to the Union, determined the appropriate value of the claim, and recommended that the U.S. House of Representatives allow, disallow, or bar the claim. Settled claims were then reported to Congress.

Claimants were required to answer a long list of questions concerning their loyalty to the union cause and their activities during the war.

Once the commission was enacted, Andrew Shell, the reverend, claimed that when Carter's men passed through Piney Flats on their way to burn the river bridges, they stole property from his farm. Shell's deposition was initially filed on Jan. 21, either 1873 or 1874. As of July 31, 1877, the case had still not been settled.

Nearly 15 years after the loss of property, Mr. S.H. Hendrix, to whom Shell had given a power of attorney, wrote Charles F. Benjamin, presumably in the claims office, and said: "Of course he (Mr. Shell) don't expect to live long, but wants his business all up square before his final departure and still has confidence that he will get justice. If there is any other evidence needed as to loyalty which he understands is the trouble please allow him to furnish it."

Eventually, the government allowed $320 of Mr. Shell's $575 claim for one gray mare, one roan horse, and one sorrel mare.

Shell's tract of land contained more than 500 acres, about four miles north of the bridge on the Watauga River at Carter's Station. He lived there from 1861 to 1865. During the war, his property was behind Confederate lines.

"I remained at home all the time could not get away," Shell said, according to a transcript of the deposition.

During the war, Shell said he went to nearby Elizabethton, where he was arrested by the command of Capt. David McClellan.

"I was compelled to take some kind of oath to be allowed to return home which I did -- Capt. McClellan was drunk," Shell said. "My life was in danger. His command was nothing better than a mob. I was well aware of the terrible ill will that the Rebel [undecipherable] had at me because of my Union sentiments."

Shell said he was known to be a Union loyalist by all who knew him; others also testified that he was loyal. He said he never participated in the Confederacy.

Shell noted that his son, Adam Clark Shell, in order to avoid being put in the Confederate army, attempted to make his way to Kentucky to join the Union. He was captured by the Confederates and taken to Richmond, Virginia, where he was placed in Castle Thunder and kept for months. Castle Thunder was operated by the Confederacy as a prison to house people from the Union.

With help, Shell said his son was released and returned home, but Confederate soldiers continued to pursue him. There was no chance that his son could reach the Union soldiers, so Shell hired a substitute for his son.

Shell said he paid $1,700 to get his son out of Piney Flats in Confederate gear. The substitute died while in the Confederate service.

Shell said Confederate authorities took eight head of horses, corn, hay, oats, cattle, and hogs from his property, according to the deposition. He also said a new wagon was taken when they were encamped nearby.

"They made a point to shout at my property as they would go through my farm on the train," Shell said. "They hated me so badly, they pretended to pay in their trash sometimes, but I never regarded it as a payment."

Shell, who said he basically quit preaching during the war, said his family was often threatened and "pistols even drawn on my sons and I have heard the music of Rebel lead near me," he said. "I have often had my property taken because of being what they called a Lincolnite."

The man said Samuel Carter's men took his horses when they were heading to the bridge at the Holston River.

"They were engaged in the taking but a short time, for just at the time the taking was done the firing commenced at the bridge on the Watauga River and Gen. Carter with all others moved off rapidly toward the firing," he said.

Carter's men had traveled from Lexington, Kentucky to Bluff City, then known as Union, on the Holston River.

"Then they burned the bridge, then they came down along the railroad to the Watauga River where the railroad crosses the river," Shell said. "There, they burned the bridge over that river passing the farm going and coming, from there they returned to Kentucky by way of Kingsport, Lee County and the Cumberland Gap."

One of his sons, Andrew Marion Shell, said he witnessed the horses being taken. The soldiers said they regretted taking the horses, but theirs had been "broken down."

Alfred Hughes said he was at the Shell farm on the day the horses were taken.

"I seen them led out of the barn lot and mount and ride them off with the command down the road towards the Watauga Bridge, seen the bridge fired, I returned home then, and left the command still at the bridge and during the night the command returned back through by [Shell's farm] and back into Kentucky."

Hiram Hughes, who lived along Main Street in Piney Flats, said he recalled seeing a federal soldier ride a sorrel horse as the brigade passed his property

"The command had encamped at and about my farm and as they passed on the next morning I seen the sorrel horse and a soldier was riding him," Hughes recalled in the deposition. "This I am not mistaken about, I understood that the command had a skirmish at the Watauga Bridge the evening before. I live about seven miles from said Watauga Bridge, and on the road that the Brigade traveled in going back into [Kentucky]."

A skirmish occurred at Carter's Depot, where 150 Union soldiers fought 130 Confederate soldiers, according to The Longest Night: A Military History of the Civil War by David J. Eicher. Carter's men burned the depot, burned a cache of supplies, and set fire to the bridge. The entire structure caught aflame and collapsed into the river, Eicher wrote.

Soldiers from both sides of the Civil War are believed to have raided other properties in Piney Flats, as well, but no battles or skirmishes were reported in the community.

CHAPTER FOUR

Wolfe Brothers

In 1880, at the age of 23, John Bunyan Wolfe, the son of Frances Marion Wolfe (1836-1921) and Winifred Shell Wolfe (1835-1909), began making furniture in a shed on his father's farm near Piney Flats. Before building furniture, the boy worked on his family's farm. He grew up near present day St. Paul United Methodist Church along Allison Road. Wolfe's father served in the Confederate Army, so he was away from home during that time. Nelle Wolfe Starnes, J. B. Wolfe's granddaughter, said he would never forget the day an entire company of soldiers came to the property and demanded food. "Tiny woman that she was, Great Grandmother stood firmly in the door and told the men, 'We have little to offer, but with what I have I will cook you a meal.' Then she added in a voice that allowed no argument, 'But no man will come into my house with a gun!'"

The soldiers placed their bayonets in the ground and went inside to eat.

During his early years as a furniture manufacturer, Wolfe had an open shed on the family farm and a lathe. His lathe, the only power tool he had, was turned by a molasses mill which he had adapted for the purpose. The

John Bunyan Wolfe (Courtesy Piney Flats Historical Society)

Workers at the Wolfe Brothers factory in Piney Flats can be seen standing outside and hanging out of the building. The factory operated for more than a century in the village. (Courtesy Piney Flats Historical Society)

source of power was a horse driven around the mill by his youngest sister, Effie. A lathe is a machine that is used primarily for shaping metal or wood. It works by rotating the workpiece around a stationary cutting tool.

By 1882, Wolfe bought a more modern six horsepower engine to replace the horse and expanded the business. After a three-foot snow in 1885 collapsed a barn owned by his grandfather, Andrew Shell, he bought the property, which is the present site of the Wolfe Brothers factory. The site was located next to the railroad in Piney Flats. Here he built his first shop. In 1888, he and his cousin Edward Hughes began making furniture under the name of Wolfe Hughes Manufacturing Company.

Starnes said that an old account book kept from 1879 through 1884 documented that the business produced all kinds of made-to-order items, including bee frames for 25 cents each, coffins for $5 to 15 a piece, bedsteads for as low as $4.50, washstands for $7.20, cribs for $2.50 and safes or cupboards for $7.50 to $12. They also made picture frames, tables, stools,

The railroad allowed the Wolfe Brothers factory to ship its home and church furnishings to customers around the country. (Courtesy Piney Flats Historical Society)

doors, or anything else of wood that might be needed for local households, Starnes wrote.

In 1889, Wolfe bought Edward Hughes' interest in the company and in 1897 his younger brother, William E. Wolfe, became a partner.

The furniture business continued to grow in the village and in 1906 he sold shares to his first cousins: Robert Shell, Edward Hughes, James I. Shell, and Arthur Shell. Since the Wolfe family retained controlling interest, the name of the business remained Wolfe Brothers Furniture Company. As the company grew, they built a larger building, employed several more workers, and bought modern machinery, Starnes wrote.

During the 1930s, Starnes wrote that the factory obtained large logs, sometimes more than four feet in diameter, to be sawn into lumber and made into finished pieces of furniture. The factory worked with large hardwood lumber, extracted from forests in the Appalachian Mountains.

Wolfe Brothers was almost destroyed by fire twice in the 20th century, once in 1917 and again in 1956. Each time, however, the damaged portion was rebuilt, and the company recovered.

The fire in 1917 destroyed the machine shop at Wolfe Brothers, according to the Kingsport News. The lost was estimated at $50,000 to $75,000. Wolfe Brothers employed some 30 people on the payroll, the newspaper reported.

Mary Wolfe, president of Wolfe Brothers and John Bunyan Wolfe's daughter, told the Johnson City Press in 1956 that the fire caused about $75,000 in damage. The lost building included the machine room, the engine room, and the dry kiln, which was full of lumber, she said. The loss was not covered by insurance. Later that same year, the burned building, which housed the milling equipment, was replaced with a building made of cinder blocks and corrugated metal. That replacement building still stands.

"We've been at it this long [68 years] and have no intentions of giving up," the president told the Bristol Herald Courier. "In fact, we're only beginning."

John Starnes, great grandson of John Bunion Wolfe, said he remembers begging his great aunt Mary Wolfe if he could just go in the factory and watch the workers in operation. She always denied his requests. He later realized she would not dare let a little child go near all of the factory's unprotected belts, shafts, and pullies. Starnes added that years later, Mary Wolfe informed him that if the fire of 1956 had not occurred, the federal government most likely would have shut the factory down because of many safety violations.

By 1956, most of the original owners were dead so the company was reorganized with Mary Wolfe as president and Charles J. Shell, son of Robert Shell, as vice president. In 1961, Vernon Wilson, son-in-law of Charles Shell, became a partner, and the company was again reorganized with Wilson as president and Mary Wolfe as secretary and treasurer.

Mary Wolfe died in 1984 and Wilson and Shell bought her interest. Wolfe Brothers was then owned and managed by Vernon Wilson and his wife, Ann Shell Wilson.

Then by 2000, factory found it difficult to locate local hardwood lumber. They purchased lumber from Venezuela in South America, but it ended up being softwood, which did not produce the quality furnishings Wolfe Brothers was known for. So leadership at the factory decided to close.

CHURCH FURNITURE BY WOLFE BROTHERS AND COMPANY, PINEY FLATS, TENNESSEE

This page features multiple pages from Wolfe Brothers catalogs, including home and church furnishings. (Courtesy John Starnes)

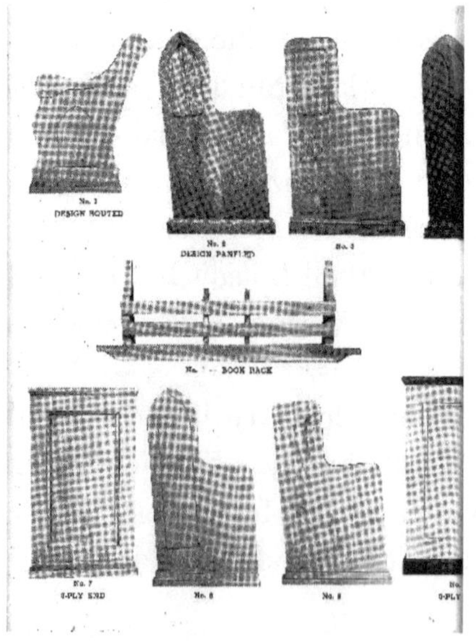

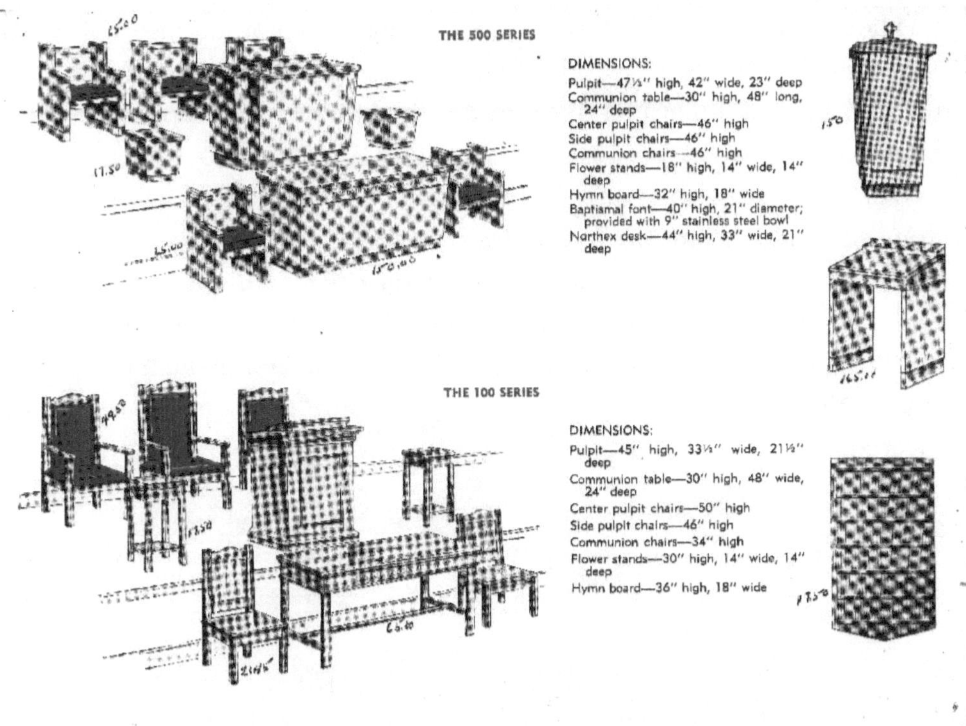

Wolfe Brothers regularly produced catalogs that provided the latest church and home furnishings. (Courtesy John Starnes)

Since then, the factory has become abandoned and dilapidated. In 2022, locals began working to preserve its history, but the building was too far gone to save. An informational marker is being planned for the site with the expectations that the building would be demolished.

A few structures from the original factory still stand in the village. Wolfe Brothers furniture can be found today in churches and homes across the region. The Piney Flats United Methodist Church, located in the village, is furnished with Wolfe Brothers products. The pews and other furniture fill the sanctuary. Some pieces of Wolfe Brothers furniture can also be found in the historic homes on Main Street, according to Mary Ann Hager, a Wolfe descendent and resident. Some residents have desks, dressers, chests, bed frames, and other unique pieces. A couple small Wolfe Brothers caskets can also be found in the village. They are now used as tables and storage chests.

The factory was, and still is, a centerpiece for the community. Every day at noon, the factory steam whistle would blow. At one time, children at Mary Hughes School all knew that this signaled the lunch bell, even more so than the school bell.

Children were also fascinated by the factory's rail cars, which were used to transport lumber into the factory for processing. It connected the saw mill up on the hill via a track that ran down to large doors that opened into

the main building. The children would take short secret rides in the cart, according to a story by the late Hildred Wolfe, the granddaughter of John Bunyan Wolfe.

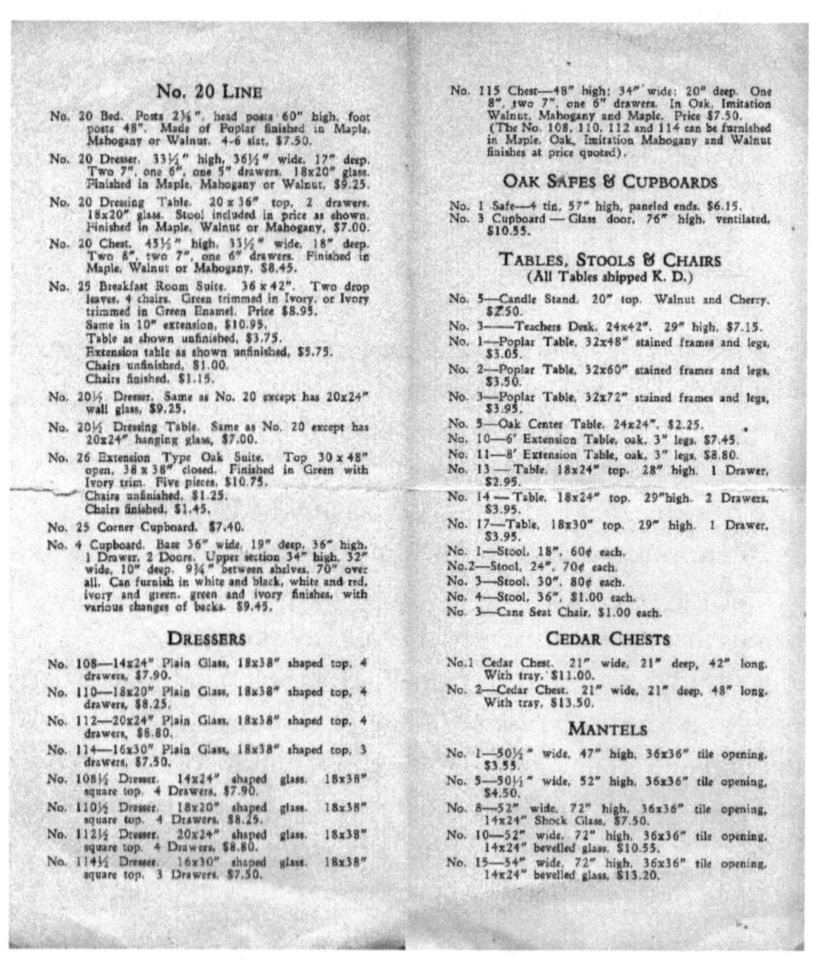

No. 20 Line

No. 20 Bed. Posts 2⅛", head posts 60" high, foot posts 48". Made of Poplar finished in Maple, Mahogany or Walnut. 4-6 slat, $7.50.

No. 20 Dresser. 33½" high, 36½" wide, 17" deep. Two 7", one 6", one 5" drawers. 18x20" glass. Finished in Maple, Mahogany or Walnut, $9.25.

No. 20 Dressing Table. 20 x 36" top, 2 drawers, 18x20" glass. Stool included in price as shown. Finished in Maple, Walnut or Mahogany, $7.00.

No. 20 Chest. 45½" high, 33½" wide, 18" deep. Two 8", two 7", one 6" drawers. Finished in Maple, Walnut or Mahogany, $8.45.

No. 25 Breakfast Room Suite. 36 x 42". Two drop leaves, 4 chairs. Green trimmed in Ivory, or Ivory trimmed in Green Enamel. Price $8.95.
Same in 10" extension, $10.95.
Table as shown unfinished, $3.75.
Extension table as shown unfinished, $5.75.
Chairs unfinished, $1.00.
Chairs finished, $1.15.

No. 20½ Dresser. Same as No. 20 except has 20x24" wall glass, $9.25.

No. 20½ Dressing Table. Same as No. 20 except has 20x24" hanging glass, $7.00.

No. 26 Extension Type Oak Suite. Top 30 x 48" open, 38 x 38" closed. Finished in Green with Ivory trim. Five pieces, $10.75.
Chairs unfinished, $1.25.
Chairs finished, $1.45.

No. 25 Corner Cupboard. $7.40.

No. 4 Cupboard. Base 36" wide, 19" deep, 36" high, 1 Drawer, 2 Doors. Upper section 34" high, 32" wide, 10" deep. 9¾" between shelves, 70" over all. Can furnish in white and black, white and red, ivory and green, green and ivory finishes, with various changes of backs. $9.45.

Dressers

No. 108—14x24" Plain Glass, 18x38" shaped top, 4 drawers, $7.90.

No. 110—18x20" Plain Glass, 18x38" shaped top, 4 drawers, $8.25.

No. 112—20x24" Plain Glass, 18x38" shaped top, 4 drawers, $8.80.

No. 114—16x30" Plain Glass, 18x38" shaped top, 3 drawers, $7.50.

No. 108½ Dresser. 14x24" shaped glass. 18x38" square top. 4 Drawers, $7.90.

No. 110½ Dresser. 18x20" shaped glass. 18x38" square top. 4 Drawers, $8.25.

No. 112½ Dresser. 20x24" shaped glass. 18x38" square top. 4 Drawers, $8.80.

No. 114½ Dresser. 16x30" shaped glass. 18x38" square top. 3 Drawers, $7.50.

No. 115 Chest

No. 115 Chest—48" high; 34" wide; 20" deep. One 8", two 7", one 6" drawers. In Oak, Imitation Walnut, Mahogany and Maple. Price $7.50.
(The No. 108, 110, 112 and 114 can be furnished in Maple, Oak, Imitation Mahogany and Walnut finishes at price quoted).

Oak Safes & Cupboards

No. 1 Safe—4 tin, 57" high, paneled ends, $6.15.
No. 3 Cupboard — Glass door, 76" high, ventilated, $10.55.

Tables, Stools & Chairs
(All Tables shipped K. D.)

No. 5—Candle Stand. 20" top. Walnut and Cherry. $2.50.
No. 3——Teachers Desk. 24x42". 29" high, $7.15.
No. 1—Poplar Table, 32x48" stained frames and legs, $3.05.
No. 2—Poplar Table, 32x60" stained frames and legs, $3.50.
No. 3—Poplar Table, 32x72" stained frames and legs, $3.95.
No. 5—Oak Center Table. 24x24". $2.25.
No. 10—6' Extension Table, oak, 3" legs, $7.45.
No. 11—8' Extension Table, oak, 3" legs, $8.80.
No. 13 — Table, 18x24" top. 28" high. 1 Drawer, $2.95.
No. 14 — Table, 18x24" top. 29" high. 2 Drawers, $3.95.
No. 17—Table, 18x30" top. 29" high. 1 Drawer, $3.95.
No. 1—Stool, 18", 60¢ each.
No. 2—Stool, 24", 70¢ each.
No. 3—Stool, 30", 80¢ each.
No. 4—Stool, 36", $1.00 each.
No. 3—Cane Seat Chair, $1.00 each.

Cedar Chests

No. 1 Cedar Chest. 21" wide, 21" deep, 42" long. With tray, $11.00.
No. 2—Cedar Chest. 21" wide, 21" deep, 48" long. With tray, $13.50.

Mantels

No. 1—50½" wide, 47" high, 36x36" tile opening, $3.55.
No. 5—50½" wide, 52" high, 36x36" tile opening, $4.50.
No. 8—52" wide, 72" high, 36x36" tile opening, 14x24" Shock Glass, $7.50.
No. 10—52" wide, 72" high, 36x36" tile opening, 14x24" bevelled glass, $10.55.
No. 15—54" wide, 72" high, 36x36" tile opening, 14x24" bevelled glass, $13.20.

This Wolfe Brothers price list is from November of 1940. (Courtesy John Starnes)

"He was Mr. Piney Flats," Mary Wolfe told the Kingsport Times-News in 1982 of John Bunyan Wolfe.

She and her cousin C.J. Shell spent most of their lives at Piney Flats and Shell said the secret of the company's longevity was quality.

"We have never knowingly made a so-called cheap product," Shell said, "We set prices where we have to set them to live."

The all-wood pews served as the company's bread and butter at about $25 a foot in 1982, according to Shell.

"We've got stuff in every county in every state east of the Mississippi," Shell said.

Rough times began to hit the company in the early 1980s.

"Demand is off bad," Shell said, citing a competitor in California that had bought out an old-line company and was marketing aggressively. The company had competition on the east coast, too, in West Virginia, though Shell said he had delivered furniture within blocks of his competitors' factory.

The company still employed about 15-20 people in the early 1980s.

Powering Piney Flats

The Wolfe Brothers company brought electricity and telephone service to Piney Flats.

The community was one of the first rural areas of East Tennessee to have electric power. After John Bunyan Wolfe began using steam to generate electricity for the factory in the very early 1900s, he ran electric lines to his own house and those of the stockholders, according to information provided by the Wolfe family.

Neighbors and friends in Piney Flats requested service so he furnished a few houses on Main Street with electricity for $1 a month upon condition that they leave their porch light burning to provide some illumination in the street.

In 1912, his son, Samuel Robert Wolfe Jr., married Bess Wexler, whose father gave her the old Hyder Mill property along the Watauga River.

The old Hyder Mill was located along the Watauga River in Piney Flats. (Courtesy Piney Flats Historical Society)

With the mill, the Wolfe family decided to use waterpower to generate electricity. By 1917, electric power had been furnished to every family in the village who requested it.

Soon, power lines were extended to outlying farms and meters were installed. To keep the village streets lighted, the Wolfe family decided to give everyone a free porch light which was not wired through the meters.

On farms where porch lights were seldom necessary, those free lights were just too much temptation to some customers who simply attached as many appliances as possible to extension cords which they ran through a window.

Eventually, the power system became so much overloaded that the old water mill could not supply the demand; therefore, the company purchased additional power through the nearby Johnson City power company. All circuits were then wired through meters.

In 1941, the Wolfe family sold the Piney Flats Electric Light Company to the Johnson City Power Board, which was eventually renamed BrightRidge.

In addition to electric service, the Wolfe Brothers company also needed telephone service. John Bunyan Wolfe and William E. Wolfe were unable to persuade either the Bristol or Johnson City telephone companies to provide telephone service to Piney Flats, so the brothers built their own company in the village in 1900. The new company had only eight party lines, and the switchboard was in John Bunyan Wolfe's home on Main Street. His wife, Nora Hughes Wolfe, usually attended the lines. In 1906, the Wolfe brothers and E.T. Burkey of the Rocky Springs community merged their companies with the Bluff City Phone Company, which was owned by James Henry.

They called the new company the Holston Telephone Company, which expanded rapidly, according to information provided by the Wolfe family. The Wolfe brothers bought Henry's and Burkey's interest and kept an office open in Bluff City but moved the main office to nearby Elizabethton. William E. Wolfe managed all of the company's technology and his wife, Margaret Cox Wolfe, managed the office.

The telephone switchboard was located in the Wolfe house in Piney Flats. (Courtesy Piney Flats Historical Society)

Service extended from Johnson City to Bristol, throughout Carter County, and into much of Johnson County. When building lines through remote mountain areas where it was difficult to take pack mules, workmen often found it necessary to travel on foot and carry equipment on their backs.

In 1926, after William E. Wolfe's failed health, the two brothers sold their telephone company to the Postal Telegraph and Telephone Company of Bristol. There was a provision in the purchase agreement that stated that customers in Piney Flats would never have to pay long distance for calls to Bristol, a provision sought by John Bunyan Wolfe.

The Village

Located just one mile from a busy four-lane highway and adjacent to a massive industrial complex lies the peaceful village of Piney Flats. The village features more than two dozen historic structures, including homes, a church, school, commercial, and industrial buildings. Most of the homes in the Piney Flats Village Historic District trace their history back to 1888, when John Bunyan Wolfe opened the Wolfe Brothers Furniture Factory beside the railroad tracks connecting Bristol and Johnson City, Tennessee.

The people who arrived in the village built several homes, including Colonial Revival, Victorian, Dutch Colonial, and bungalow-style homes. They also built general stores, churches, and the original Mary Hughes

There are two welcome signs in the Piney Flats Historic District. (Courtesy Piney Flats Historical Society)

School, which local resident and Piney Flats Historical Society founder Mary Ann Hager said has withstood fires and school consolidation over the years.

The village, which was listed on the National Register of Historic Places in November of 2011, is practically bookended by Mary Hughes School, which was founded in 1897, and the Piney Flats United Methodist Church, built in 1914.

While the historic district consists of dozens of original structures, several others have been lost over the years, either through demolition, dilapidation, or disaster.

Mary Hughes School, the largest building in the village, is located at 240 North Austin Springs Road, near its intersection with Piney Flats Road. It's a two-story structure constructed of brick and features a cross-gable roof of asphalt shingles. A small portico at the main entrypoint to the school is covered by a pediment and is supported by two large white columns.

The history of Mary Hughes School began after the Civil War when the first school in Piney Flats was held in a former slave cabin on the property of Samuel DeVault Hughes, according to a NRHP nomination form. By 1873, classes moved to Shell's Chapel, the Union Church of the community, where they were held until 1887.

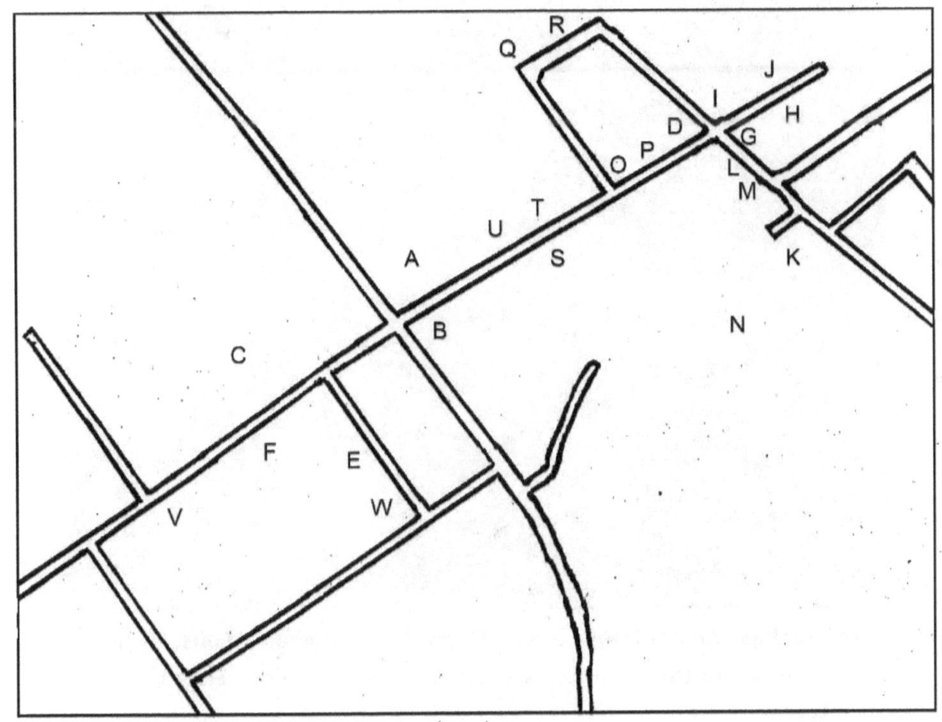

Map of Piney Flats Historic District

A. Hughes House, Main St.

B. Simerly House, Main St.

C. Mary Hughes School, Main St.

D. John Bunyan Wolfe House, Main St.

E. Masengill House, High St.

F. Community center, Main St.

G. Carr store, Mountain View Dr.

H. Carr houses, Main St.

I. Sam Hughes House, Main St.

J. Ford House, Main St.

K. Wolfe Brothers Factory

L. Planer Shop, Mountain View Dr.

M. Post Office, Mountain View Dr.

N. Jim Shell House, Wolfe Brothers Rd.

O. K. McKamey House, Main St.

P. Ben McKamey House, Main St.

Q. Bob Shell House, Methodist Church St.

R. Piney Flats U.M.C., Methodist Church St.

S. Bess Wolfe House, Wolfe Brothers Rd.

T. Richard Smalling House, Main St.

U. Quaintance & Gilmer homes, Main St.

V. Cole House, Main St.

W. David Hughes House, Huffman Hill Rd.

Mary Hughes and her family are pictured here in the late 1800s. Hughes is the namesake of the community's school. (Courtesy Piney Flats Historical Society)

In 1894, Samuel Hughes and his wife, Mary Hughes, donated one and one-half acres of land for the purpose of erecting a brick school building at least 40 feet wide and 60 feet long. Residents in Piney Flats immediately began constructing the new school, which they named Mary Hughes Institute, in honor of Samuel Hughes's wife. The school was built of brick made on site.

The new school was administered by a local school board and students were charged tuition which ranged from $1.00 per month for grades one and two, up to $2.00 for month for advanced subjects in the upper grades through tenth.

"Mary Hughes Institute (so named for the splendid lady whose generous husband started the enterprise) stands as a monument to the liberality and progressive spirit of the people of this community," a 1911 school catalog states.

These two images show Mary Hughes School then and now. The top historic photograph features one of its classes. The bottom photograph was taken more recently. Expansions, fires, and other events have changed Mary Hughes School over the years. It continues to serve Piney Flats as an elementary school, although it previously also housed middle school and high school students. (Courtesy Piney Flats Historical Society)

If they did not already reside in Piney Flats, students that attended the institution were able to find board in the village. It cost boys and girls $10 and $12 per month for boarding. The school featured ten grades and students were required to have a grade of 80 percent to pass to the next grade level.

In 1920, Mary Hughes became a three-year high school, and by 1923, it became a four-year high school. The first addition in 1924 included four classrooms and an auditorium. The school featured one of the region's first gymnasiums in 1929. Members of the community donated money, materials, and labor to construct the gymnasium.

Tragedy struck Piney Flats when fire destroyed the school. In the 1930s and in 1940, the school's parent teacher association had raised money to purchase books that burned in a fire at the school on April 11, 1941. The fire destroyed the original building along with the 1924 addition. Almost immediately after, Alley Construction of Bristol was hired to build a new school, which cost about $108,128. High school classes met in the gymnasium during the 1941-1942 school year. Elementary classes were held in a storage building at the Wolfe Brothers factory.

A large gymnasium, a cafeteria, and a Masonic Hall were added in 1949. Then, in 1953, six classrooms and a library were added to the school, but those were completely lost to a fire in 1956. Fortunately, wind direction and luck favored the local citizens who came to fight the fire, and the remainder of Mary Hughes School was saved. For the rest of the 1956-1957 school year, classes which had been meeting in the structures that burned, were held at the Piney Flats Union Church. The destroyed classrooms and library were rebuilt in 1957 and enlarged in 1960 and 1962.

In 1968, high schools in Sullivan County were consolidated and Mary Hughes ceased operation as a high school but continued to be operated as an elementary school and middle school. In the early 21st century, the historic Mary Hughes School continues to operate as an elementary school, and middle and high school students travel outside of Piney Flats to attend classes.

The small town of Piney Flats has always been supportive of the various athletics programs at Mary Hughes School.

Athletics at Mary Hughes School have always been popular extra-curricular activities. The 1931 men's basketball team at Mary Hughes is in the bottom photograph and the women's basketball team from 1936 is in the top photograph. (Courtesy Piney Flats Historical Society and Janie Torbett)

Mary Hughes School in Piney Flats has welcomed elementary, middle, and high school aged children. Children are pictured in the early 1930s in the top photograph and the school's safety team from about 1950 is in the bottom photograph. (Courtesy Piney Flats Historical Society and Janie Torbett)

Fire damaged Mary Hughes School in 1956. (Courtesy Janie Torbett)

The girls basketball team at Mary Hughes had an outstanding season in 1936. There are some reports that claim the team won the state championship at a tournament in Knoxville. Others say there was no statewide tournament, but it was a regional championship. In any case, however, when the team returned from Knoxville, there was a large crowd to cheer and greet them when their train pulled in at the Piney Flats depot.

A community center, owned by the county school system, and a park are located across the street along Austin Springs Road from the school. The park was established in 1935 and features trees, shrubs, unique rock outcroppings, and a concrete picnic table. There's also a stone monument that was constructed in the mid-1930s. A concrete plaque on the monument states: "THESE GROUNDS DONATED BY S.D. AND MARY HUGHES SEPT 28, 1894."

Samuel Hughes died in 1897 and his wife Mary Hughes died in 1880. They are buried at the cemetery at New Bethel Presbyterian Church.

Mary Hughes

Hughes marker in Piney Flats near Mary Hughes School.
(Photo by author)

"Mrs. Mary Hughes, wife of Mr. Samuel Hughes, and daughter of Lawrence Bowers, Esq., of this county died, last Friday night at her home ear Shell's dept. For many years had been an exemplary member of the Baptist church and died as she had lived—a Christian," the Jonesborough Journal reported.

Several smaller brick and clapboard sided historic homes can be found to the south of Mary Hughes School along Austin Springs Road. Dr. Aaron Cole's bungalow is located at 283 N. Austin Springs Road. It was constructed in 1935. The doctor, who birthed many Piney Flats babies and cared for dozens of families over the years, worked out of his home, but also made house calls.

Piney Flats physician Aaron often visited homes by foot, horse, and car. (Top photo by author, bottom photo courtesy Piney Flats Historical Society)

"He delivered many of us in our parents' or grandparents' homes," said Phyllis Ford, who remembered Dr. Cole. "He had a small office down the road from our house and each fall I took the slowest, smallest steps I could take walking to his office for my yearly 'cold shot,' I have never heard of a 'cold shot' since those days and I always had a cold anyway. I can still remember the medicinal odor one got when walking into his office."

The doctor was born on May 27, 1886, in Goin, a small community near Tazewell, Tennessee. Cole taught school for six years and in 1918 he married one of his students, Hassie Anne Keck. He later decided to attend medical school and opened his practice in Goin after graduation.

Cole moved to Piney Flats in 1925 and established his office, where he practiced medicine for 35 years. Cole said he delivered about 6,500 babies during his 44 years of practice.

Like other country doctors, Cole made house calls at all hours of the day and during all types of weather. He was often called to pull teeth and treat animals.

Cole rode a horse to make many of his calls, but in 1915 he purchased a Model T automobile to speed his travels. The roads at the time were often muddy and impassable for a car. He would often ride his horse into the 1920s and 1930s because the horse was more reliable.

Mrs. Virginia "Pet" Deakins Houston also said Cole made his medical house calls by horseback.

Another historic home is located at the corner of Austin Springs Road and Huffman Road. The McClellan House, which was once owned by Michael Dallas Masengill of the Rocky Mount Masengill family, was built in 1903. Some of the homes along N. Austin Springs Road may have originally been constructed for workers of the Wolfe Brothers Furniture Company.

Nearby High Street, which connects N. Austin Springs Road and Huffman Hill Road, features a variety of homes, including 20th century mobile homes, small bungalows and cottages, and historic Victorians. As late as the mid 1900s, old deeds reveal that High Street was once known as Kidd Street.

The white clapboard sided home at 350 High Street was built around 1900. Recognized as the Masengill House in early 20th century deeds, this old house has been meticulously restored. This home has a twin on Main Street.

Feathers were once stored in the floor of the David Hughes House in Piney Flats. This home is located on Huffman Hill Road. (Photo by author)

The home at 241 Huffman Hill Road, on the corner at High Street, may be the oldest residence in Piney Flats. The home has been modified; however, it still features a great bit of original detail. David Hughes constructed this home about 1800. He stored feathers in space that could be reached through a trap door in the floor, according to descendants.

He kept a store at his home, selling buttons, bar iron, overalls, bacon, flour, cotter-molds, peach brandy, and salt, according to the late Nelle Wolfe Starnes. He often accepted feathers in trade for items. Some local settlers often came to his home to have Hughes write legal documents, Starnes added. Prominent pioneers, including the Alisons, Masengills, Torbetts, and DeVaults, were among those to use Hughes' services.

Hughes, a Revolutionary War veteran who fought at the Battle of Kings Mountain, is believed to have settled in the Piney Flats area in 1774-1775, according to Dawn of Tennessee Valley and Tennessee History, which was written by historian Samuel Cole Williams. He also became involved in local issues; he supported the Washington District, which was located in Northeast Tennessee, being annexed by North Carolina, and the first local grand jury. Hughes, who owned a large amount of land in Piney Flats, is buried at New Bethel Cemetery.

Piney Flats Road parallels High Street and crosses Main Street and Austin Springs Road. It connects nearby U.S. Highway 11E, the village and the nearby community of Watauga in Carter County. The historic district includes a few properties on Piney Flats Road.

The one-story brick residence at 457 Piney Flats Road is known as the Kyle McKamey House. It was built in 1937 and features English Cottage Revival architecture. McKamey, who died in 1966, worked at Summers Hardware in nearby Johnson City.

The two-story Opal and Mamie Shell House is located down the street at 472 Piney Flats Road. Described as an I-house, this home was built in 1900. It also features a one-story barn built in 1900. The one-story Hicks House was built in 1900 at 492 Piney Flats Road. It features several outbuildings, including a barn, corn crib, and wash house, all built in 1900.

The brick bungalow property at 376 Piney Flats Road is known as the Browder House. It is located outside of the official historic district. An earlier home had burned down at the back of the property, according to a recent owner, Marshall Young. Its replacement was constructed in 1932 for the Browder family. Unfortunately, Mrs. Browder died before she was able to have any children and her husband later remarried.

When the Browders died, the house went up for silent auction, Young said. A local woman had always loved the home and asked her husband to place a bid. They won and moved in. Another family eventually bought the home and made some modifications. The Young family later bought the home and sold it in 2021.

"We have updated the home drastically but tried to maintain the house's character," Young said before selling the property.

Two-lane Main Street stretches for about one-half mile through the middle of the Piney Flats Historic District. It is lined with late 19th century and early 20th century homes, many of which have been preserved for future generations.

The Simerly House is also known as the Hal Massengill House. (Photo by author)

The grand Simerly House is located at 208 Main Street near Piney Flats Road. Also known as the Massengil House, the white clapboard-sided Queen Anne residence was built in 1909. The three-story home features a brick foundation, a wrap-around porch with sawn balusters and a hip-roofed dormer, according to an entry in the National Register of Historic Places. The home, which features restored moldings and door hardware, is practically identical to the home at 350 High Street. For many years in the late 20th century the Simerly House had been vacant and deteriorated. The Simerly family purchased the home in 2009, which had been restored by the Hunigan family.

The Hughes House stands across the street at 217 Main Street. This unique Queen Anne home was built in 1888. With a large front porch, the two-story home has weatherboard covering and features a rectangular turret and front bay window. A large addition was constructed to the left of the original home in 1907. Jim and Mary Ann Hager bought the home in 1999

The Hughes House is located on Main Street in Piney Flats. This home has been expanded since this photo was taken. (Courtesy Piney Flats Historical Society)

and restored the entire structure. They also added a large carriage house featuring a garage and upstairs apartment.

A one and half story residence at 235 Main Street was constructed about 1943. Known on the Historic Register as the Quaintance House, the brick residence features a bay window and an asphalt shingle gable roof. Next door, the Gilmer House is located at 245 Main Street. It's also known as the Wilbur Smalling House and was built in 1933, according to the historic register. The one and one-half story bungalow was remodeled in 2006. The home also features an original two-story washhouse, recently used for storage, at the rear of the property. From 1949 to 1957, the property served as the parsonage for the Piney Flats United Methodist Church. The church had acquired the property from Wilbur Smalling.

The beautiful bungalow at 250 Main Street was built in 1932. Known as the Bess Wolfe House, or Starnes House, this one and one-half story features several original outbuildings. The main house has a brick veneer with stone addition. The outbuildings include a 1940s garage, a 1950 storage building, 1940 tool shed and a smokehouse and well house built in 1932. The well house still includes pulleys for pulling a water bucket.

The Bess Wolfe House was built in 1932 in Piney Flats along Main Street. (Photo by author)

The Richard Smalling House is located on Main Street in Piney Flats. (Photo by author)

The Richard Trivett House, or Robert Smalling House, is located across the street at 253 Main Street. The side gable house with Queen Anne influence was built in 1910. It's a two-story residence. Two original outbuildings, built in 1910, can be found behind the house, including a one-story smokehouse and dairy, and a one-story barn.

Look closely, and one might spot where an old general store once stood. A small shop was located close to the road, adjacent to the home at 253 Main Street.

The ranch style home at 273 Main Street, known as the Landreth House, was built in 1953. A two-story barn, constructed in 1910, is on the property. It was originally used for hay storage and for drying tobacco.

Another historic home, the Knack McKamey House, is located at 289 Main Street at the corner of Main and McKamey Street. The Queen Anne cottage was built in 1932. Nearby, the Roger Feathers House was built in 1933. The one-story frame house, located at 292 Main Street, was damaged by fire, but still stands along Main Street. The Queen Anne two-story frame house at 295 Main Street

The Knack McKamey House is pictured above. It is located adjacent to the Benjamin McKamey House, which is pictured below. Both homes are located on Main Street in Piney Flats. (Photos by author)

76

A sidewalk and wrought iron fence can be seen in front of John Bunyan Wolfe House.
(Photo at top courtesy Piney Flats Historical Society, photo below by author)

was built in 1903. It's known as the Pyron House and Benjamin McKamey House. The property includes a smokehouse built in 1903.

John Bunyan Wolfe's home, built in 1905, is located next door at 317 Main Street. It's listed on the historic register as the Landreth-Thomas House. The two- and one-half story frame house with weatherboard is of Queen Anne design. The property also features a wellhouse, garage, and smokehouse, all built in 1909. The smokehouse was moved about 10 feet from its original location, according to the historic register. A beautiful black wrought iron fence can be found in front of the house, as well as an original brick sidewalk.

The Sam D. Hughes House at 327 Main Street is the only Dutch Colonial Revival house in Piney Flats. Its gambrel roof, which is a symmetrical two-sided roof with two slopes on each side, is typical of Dutch architecture. The two-story structure with clapboard siding on the façade and rear, and Hardie-board on both sides, was built about 1938.

Two bungalows, built in 1930, can be found across the street at 336 Main Street and 344 Main Street. Brothers Ben Carr and Mitchell Carr built the brick Arts and Crafts bungalows.

Sam Hughes House pictured in top photo. The Mitchell and Ben Carr homes are below. (Photos by author)

The Ford House is located at the end of Main Street in the village of Piney Flats. Ford was a successful businessman. (Photo by author)

"B.L." Ford (Courtesy Emily Holmberg)

The Hamilton House or Ford House is located at 339 Main Street. This large two-story frame house with weatherboard walls was built in 1900. It includes two brick chimneys, a bay window and a wraparound porch with wood columns. A two-story addition was built in 1981. The property also includes a garage built in 1900.

The Ford House is named after Burton Lafayette "B.L." Ford, a successful Piney Flats businessman. He owned a general store and a canning factory in the village. His family was often mentioned in the newspaper society columns as they traveled to Knoxville, visited the Boring community, or when one of the children was nearly struck by a train near their home. He died at age of 41 of typhoid fever in 1910, according to newspaper reports. After he died, the family moved out of state. His daughter, Viola Pauline Ford, eventually became a popular teacher and principal in Bristol, Tennessee.

Narrow Methodist Church Street and McKamey Street create half a loop around the west side of Main Street. The Bob Shell House, located at 349 McKamey Street, was built in 1910. The home features a gabled ell with a bungalow porch, according to the Historic Register. It's a one and one-half story frame house with a raised basement. There's also a historic concrete post fence at the front of the property, built in 1911, and a two-story barn with hay loft, built in 1923. A one-story tool shed, built in 1923, is also on the Shell property.

The Piney Flats United Methodist Church previously served as the Piney Flats Union Church and was home to several denominations. (Courtesy Piney Flats Historical Society).

80

Several stained-glass windows have been installed at Piney Flats United Methodist Church. (Photo by author)

The historic Piney Flats United Methodist Church, previously known as the Piney Flats Union Church, is located at 225 Methodist Church Street. The red brick church, with beautiful stained-glass windows and high vaulted ceilings, is the successor of the community's first church, Shell's Chapel, which was established in 1873.

In December 1913, the members of Shell's Chapel "dared to pull up stakes and move to the present site," according to a 1950 dedication pamphlet. "They dared to build when it became apparent such was the proper procedure for greater service.

Known as the Piney Flats Union Church, the new church structure was more imposing than the small weatherboard Shell's Chapel, according to a written history of the church. It was larger and was made of solid brick. Its stained-glass windows were installed as memorials to honor former members:

B.L. Ford, Andrew Shell and one donated by Drusilla Langdon for A. B. Parmelee and C. M. Parmelee.

Piney Flats United Methodist Church has seen several expansions over the years. The church's belfry –the structure housing the bell -- originally had crenellations, giving it an appearance of Norman architecture, but they

The choir performs at Piney Flats United Methodist Church in the top photo. The church cemetery can be seen in the bottom photo. (Top courtesy Janie Torbett, bottom photo by author)

82

were removed in 1972, according to the National Register of Historic Places.

Beulah Smalling was solely responsible for raising the money to buy the bell for the belfry, according to a written church history. She was chosen to ring the bell to call the worshipers to the first service held in the new building. She was so tiny and the pull of the rope so strong that she found herself swinging all the way to the ceiling. But she held on and came down safely, the church history states.

The church's south addition was constructed in 1949, which led the congregation to host a dedication ceremony. A portico and stairs were then built in 1952. A northern addition was built in 1991 and a western addition, which contains a gymnasium, was built in 2002.

The church's pews were constructed of solid oak, and because of their shape and the slope of the floor, every single one had to be constructed for the exact spot on which it was to be placed. They were made and donated by the nearby Wolfe Brothers factory with loving care because most of the men who worked there were also members of the church. The altar, also of the finest oak, was painstakingly turned and fitted by E.W. Hughes.

The Shell Cemetery, located at 228 Methodist Church Street, can be found on elevated ground adjacent the church. This large historic cemetery began with the burial of Reverend Andrew Shell, a Piney Flats settler. Several families, including the Hughes, Torbetts, and McKameys are buried here.

Mountain View Drive intersects Main Street near the Bunyan property. A short section of Mountain View Drive connects Main Street with the nearby railroad before heading north through the industrial park and U.S. Highway 19W.

The former Mitchell Carr General Store is located at 305 Mountain View Drive. This one story, frame construction building, was built in 1939. It was fashioned as a general store and features white weatherboard. Today, the front of the store features a small front porch and the words "GENERAL STORE" emboss the façade.

Carr's store made most of its money selling items for local farms. Like other local stores, it also had a variety of grocery items and other household necessities. The store served as a meeting place for local farmers who would share news and enjoy one another's company.

Mitchell Carr operated a store in this building in the village. The property, now own by the Simerly family, has the words "GENERAL STORE" embossed on the façade. (Photo by author)

Furnishings inside included a long glass counter near the front, and a pot-bellied stove near the center. The stove was surrounded by a number of empty nail kegs, an RC cola bench, and some wood stools that were manufactured nearby at the Wolfe Brothers factory. Local farmers often assembled at those stools, moving them outside during the summer. Vinegar was stored in a wooden barrel and coal oil was stored in a 250-gallon steel tank. The kerosene – a staple often used to help start early morning stove fires -- was sold by the gallon which was dispensed by a single "pump from the tank, the according to the Piney Flats Historical Society.

Carr served on the Sullivan County Board of Education, resulting in gatherings at the shop where the superintendent, Carr, and others discussed serious issues of the importance to the area school system.

The Carr store remained in the family until 1981, when Roy Baker acquired the building, according to the Piney Flats Historical Society. Baker named it the General Store and operated it for a short time. He ultimately

84

Bob Meyers operated a store on Main Street in Piney Flats. (Courtesy Piney Flats Historical Society)

sold the building to the Wayne Snodgrass family in 1984. It's no longer operating as a store, but still displays the name outside. John and Vicky Simerly acquired the property in 2017, according to tax records.

Other stores in the village included Bob Meyers' store on Main Street. It was across from the historic Hughes House and adjacent to a barbershop. Meyers store was similar to the Mitchell Carr Store and also featured a soda counter. Neither the store nor the barbershop buildings still stand. Another general store and gas station once operated in a white clapboard sided building across from Mary Hugh School.

The SR Wolfe Machine Shop is located nearby in a red frame building at 314 Mountain View Drive. Also known as the John Landreth Property, the front-gable building was built in 1900. There's a white door and a sign above, which states "Wolfe Bros Planer Mill." A planer mill is a facility that takes cut and seasoned boards from a sawmill and turns them into finished

John Bunyan Wolfe operated a machine shop in this building in Piney Flats. It also served as the planer building for his factory. (Photo by author)

dimensional lumber. When the Wolfe Brothers factory was operating, lumber was finished in the planer mill.

As more of the milling operations were concentrated next to the original factory, the building became John Bunyan Wolfe's personal machine shop. He undertook mechanical projects that would, if successful, be incorporated into the operations at the nearby factory.

The building continues to be used as a machine shop today. Nearby, there's also a one-story coal yard scale house that was built in 1900.

Piney Flats has been home to multiple post office buildings over the years. One built in the mid-20th century can be found next to the planer mill at 318 Mountain View Drive. This front-gable building features an erroneous sign. It states: Old Piney Flats Post Office 1860. It was actually

These two photos show two different post offices in Piney Flats' history. (Courtesy Piney Flats Historical Society)

built in 1960. This building was constructed in front of the community's first post office. Andrew Shell served as the first postmaster. Rural free delivery began in 1901 with two carriers, Charles Warren and Robert Smalling, and a substitute carrier, John Anderson. The two mail routes included most of the area between the Holston and the Watauga rivers.

Piney Flats has been home to multiple Post Office buildings. These photos were taken when the buildings were located in the historic village. The Post Office moved to Jonesboro Road off U.S. Highway 11E in the late 20th century.
(Courtesy Piney Flats Historical Society)

Another Piney Flats bungalow can be found at 349 Mountain View Drive. The Dyes House was built in 1933, according to the Historic Register. This two-story brick house also features a wash house, constructed in 1933. There's also a smokehouse and a garage, both built in 1933.

The railroad runs north and south through Piney Flats. On the other side of the railroad, a few historic properties can be found on Tank Hill Road and Wolfe Brothers Road.

Ben Carr operated a store in 1900 in a two-story frame house known as the Lomax House. It's located at 405 and directly faces the railroad. The building features weatherboard and tar paper walls, as well as stone and cinder block piers. Also featuring a covered front porch, the Lomax House is now deteriorating and is surrounded by a wood fence.

The old Wolfe Brothers factory is located nearby at 562 Wolfe Brothers Road. Wolfe chose the location because of its proximity to the railroad. In 1886, he purchased the land, which had belonged to his grandfather. He then moved his furniture business from his farm to help establish the Wolfe Brothers factory.

The Wolfe Brothers factory is located near the railroad in the village of Piney Flats. (Courtesy John Starnes)

This Wolfe Brothers sign once could be seen outside of the factory in Piney Flats. (Photo by author)

In recent decades, the two-story wood frame manufacturing building has deteriorated. A Bluff City businessman purchased the property in 2021, but it's unknown what will happen to the historic site. A one-story milling building is located nearby. It was built in 1956.

The Jim Shell House is located a bit further up the street at 564 Wolfe Brothers Road. The bungalow house with arts and crafts influence was

The Jim Shell House was built in 1920 near the Wolfe Brothers factory. A sidewalk connects the home to the railroad. (Photo by author)

constructed in 1920. It's a one and one-half story brick house with a brick and concrete foundation, according to the Historic Register. Several historic outbuildings are also on the property, including corn crib, well house, and hen house, all built in 1920. The large three-story barn on the property was constructed in 1950. Look closely and one might also see the long sidewalk that stretches from the home's front entrance to the nearby railroad. The sidewalk is now overgrown.

Early pioneer Andrew Shell built his home near the Jim Shell House in a hollow at the rear of the property. The beautiful two-story brick home was destroyed by fire and has since been demolished.

Attorney visits Piney Flats

In June of 1930, Samuel Price, a Johnson City attorney, spoke at a cemetery decoration program at the former Union Church in Piney Flats. More than 1,000 people listened to him as he spoke about the community's important connections with the development of Tennessee, according to newspaper articles on the event.

Price spoke of the Watauga Association and the state of Franklin, two early Tennessee government organizations. He also mentioned William Blount, who lived for a short time at nearby Rocky Mount. He noted that "scores of people" visited Rocky Mount and the Cobb house each year—long before it became a designated state historic site.

Price referred to the sterling characteristics of the pioneer citizens of Piney Flats and of the hardships with which they had to endure. The rapid development of the territory, after the arrival of Blount, was also explained in detail by the speaker.

Blount spent much of his time at Rocky Mount conducting work for the Southwest Territory.

Price was a prominent local attorney during the first half of the 20th century. He also served on several area boards, including Milligan College

Rural Piney Flats

The community of Piney Flats stretches far outside of the boundary lines of the village historic district. While many families settled in the village, others received land grants and purchased hundreds of acres of land across the Forks--the area between the Watauga and Holston rivers--as early as the mid-1700s. As families moved in, residents began to build homes, churches, schools, and country stores.

This area, which covers about 30-square miles, is home to numerous smaller communities, hamlets, and crossroads. Take a look at any map, or while traveling down some of the community's back roads, and one will find dozens of place names. Rural mail carriers and postal stations, however, create a common bond for these Piney Flats communities that make up the 37686 zip code.

Postman James Trivett oftentimes delivered mail in rural Piney Flats by horse and wagon. Several communities in the Piney Flats area had their own Post Office locations. (Courtesy Janie Torbett)

The communities of Edgefield and New Bethel are located along Pickens Bridge Road, which connects Piney Flats with nearby Boones Creek in Washington County. Some documents refer to this area as Alison Forest and the Old Forks. They are home to some of Piney Flats' most notable families, such as the Alisons, Torbetts, Kings, Mottern, and Warrens. New Bethel Presbyterian Church, which is one of the state's oldest congregations, is located in this section of Piney Flats.

Poplar Ridge, Weaver Branch, and Hunting Hill can be found just north of the village near Bluff City. Here, residents established one of the most successful cheese factories in Tennessee. Members of the King, Warren, Webb, and Houston families also called these areas home.

The Rocky Springs, Enterprise, and Cross communities are located further north and west of the village. The Cross family, one of Piney Flats' earliest pioneer families, lived here and flourished. Families in these communities operated schools, churches, and businesses. Other families here included the DeVaults, Drokes, and Crussells.

Two more communities, Deerlick and Haw Ridge, are located near present-day Boone Dam and the site where the Watauga and Holston rivers meet. The Geisler family was especially prominent in this section of Piney Flats. They operated a successful general store at Deerlick. Other families included the Millhorns and Hodges.

A portion of Piney Flats, known as Fairview, stretches across Boone Lake toward Blountville and the Sullivan County courthouse. The communities of Austin Springs and Watauga Flats, which are partially within the Johnson City limits, are south of the village. Three sparsely populated communities--Thompson Hollow, Lick Creek, and Huffman Hollow--are located in the knobs to the east and south of the village.

New Bethel Church and Cemetery

The New Bethel Presbyterian Church is among the oldest congregations in the state of Tennessee and its cemetery's earliest grave dates back to the late 18th century. It was organized during the Revolutionary War, according

New Bethel Presbyterian Church is among the oldest congregations in Tennessee. Its history dates back to the late 18th century. (Courtesy Piney Flats Historical Society)

to written histories of the church. The beautiful brick facility sits along New Bethel Road, about four miles from the Piney Flats Historic District.

The first members of the New Bethel congregation were followers of the Reverend Dr. Joseph Rhea, a pastor of the Piney Creek Presbyterian Church in Maryland. Rhea had served in the Revolutionary War and told his congregation in Maryland about relocating to Tennessee. Before he was able to begin preaching in Tennessee; however, Rhea died in 1777. The Reverend Charles Cummings of Abingdon, Virginia, later came to Piney Flats and established a place to worship. It was destroyed two years later, according to the church's history.

Finally, in 1782, Reverend Samuel Doak, a legendary and influential minister, organized New Bethel Presbyterian Church. It was named in honor of Bethel Church in Staunton, Virginia, where he spent his early years. Doak was a well-known pastor, having established 25 churches and institutions, including Tusculum University in nearby Greene County, Tennessee. He also assisted the Overmountain Men that traveled to South Carolina to fight the British, praying with the men at nearby Sycamore Shoals in Elizabethton.

President Theodore Roosevelt once wrote of Doak as walking behind an old gray horse loaded with a sack full of books, crossing the Allegheny Mountains along the blazed trails to the Holston settlements. The stern, God-fearing teacher became a powerful influence for good.

A horse and wagon can be seen outside New Bethel Presbyterian Church in Piney Flats. (Courtesy John Starnes)

The old New Bethel School is pictured here before 1900. It was a clapboard frame structure. (Courtesy Piney Flats Historical Society)

The first New Bethel church building was made of logs and was also used as a schoolhouse for local children. Peter Williams taught school at New Bethel in 1975, church and school records show. A school existed at New Bethel through the mid-20th century.

The structure had a shingle roof and a stone chimney at the east end, according to the church's history. The pulpit was in the west end, around which the male portion of the congregation gathered. The women and the children occupied the east end near the chimney.

New Bethel's church membership grew, requiring the congregation to build an addition. In 1838, members built a hand-hewn log addition, joining to the west end. This placed the pulpit in the middle of the church. The building served the needs of the church until 1879, when the present brick building was constructed. The face of the church has changed over the years.

Recently, an education building was constructed, and the sanctuary was remodeled.

Many Presbyterian ministers have preached from the pulpit. In 1978, New Bethel called its first full-time minister, and in 1979, the new manse was completed and dedicated.

New Bethel's historic cemetery features soldiers from the Revolutionary War, the War of 1812, the Mexican war, and the American Civil War. There are more than 1,300 people buried at the cemetery, according to burial records.

Those buried at New Bethel include John Allison, a Revolutionary War captain who died in 1832; William R. Geisler and his wife Edna King Geisler, who operated a large farm, store, and blacksmith shop in western Piney Flats in the 19th century; and the cemetery's first grave which identifies the deceased as "unknown traveler," and dates back to 1790. Members from several prominent Piney Flats families, including Carr, Allison, Torbett, Milhorn, Geisler, Warren, King, Anderson, and Hughes, are buried at the cemetery.

Hundreds of people are buried at the cemetery at New Bethel Presbyterian Church. (Photo by author)

Several unique graves can be found at the New Bethel cemetery, including the first grave from 1790 of the unknown traveler. John Alison, a Revolutionary War soldier, and pioneer Hiram Hughes are also buried here. (Photos by author)

Edgefield United Methodist Church started around 1800 and sits along Pickens Bridge Road in Piney Flats. (Courtesy Janie Torbett)

Edgefield United Methodist Church

Several schools and churches have sat at the current site of the Edgefield United Methodist Church, an historic site along Pickens Bridge Road. The church started around the year 1800, according to Pastor Estel Williams. Tradition states that the first house of worship at Edgefield was constructed at that time on land belonging to the Torbetts, one of the community's most prominent families. The church was called Torbett Chapel and the Torbett Meeting House.

The property was deeded to the Methodist church in January of 1847 by the heirs of John Torbett: Catherine, Sarah, Hugh, James, and Allen Torbett, according to a church history. Several Piney Flats leaders served as the first trustees, including Andrew Shell, Abraham Gregg, Washington Borden, T.J. Newton, Isaac DeVault, Thomas Hughes, Worley Embree, James Torbett and Jesse Allison.

The original Edgefield church building, constructed of local logs, which stood a few yards northeast of where the present building stands, was torn down around 1875. The congregation constructed a new brick building in 1876 and dedicated in 1883 by the Reverend George D. French.

A new sanctuary and a renovated addition were dedicated at Edgefield in August 1950, according to an article in the Johnson City Press. The new building also featured a basement and new façade. The addition was made to the building constructed in 1876, the newspaper said.

During the early years, the church was also called Locust Grove, likely in conjunction with the Locust Grove School, which once stood on the site of the cemetery.

The church's oldest available record is from July 29, 1883. There were 42 people present that day. The earliest record of a pastor that can be established is 1883, when Pastor J.R. Cunningham delivered a sermon on November 25.

The Alison family

Descendants of the Alison family have had two homes added to the National Register of Historic Places, including the Finlay Alison House. The brick home is located along Pickens Bridge Road and is surrounded by acres of farmland. It is set on a well-manicured yard, and an extensive greenhouse operation, belonging to the owner, is behind the home. The house is a story-and a-half brick structure with a raised basement, according to the National Register of Historic Places. Unusual for the area are the interior chimneys and the cornice, the nomination form states. Bracket trim on the front porch suggests that the porch was added in the 1870s or 1880s. More recently, a small back wing and porch were added, and more ornamental iron window boxes were placed under the front windows.

The interior plan of the house consists of a central hall with a stairway to the upper story. To one side of the hall is a single room the depth of the house. The basement has a large fireplace which may have served as the original kitchen.

The NRHP says the small, compact house is important architecturally because both its form and its woodwork are exceptional for the area.

No written documentation has been found to prove when it was built, but descendants believe the Finlay Alison House was constructed in 1811, according to the nomination form.

Alison family members were early settlers in the area who became prominent and prosperous figures, as evidenced by the fact that two of the most architecturally significant structures in Sullivan County are early Alison homes. The Jesse Alison House, which was once listed on the National Register of Historic Places, has been demolished. The Allison name can be found across Piney Flats in street names and subdivisions, such as Allison Woods, Allison Timbers, and Allison Heights.

The Alison family first came to the area around 1774 when John Alison Sr. settled near New Bethel Presbyterian Church. One family member, John Alison I, also known as Captain Jack Alison, served in the Battle at Kings Mountain under General Isaac Shelby.

Torbett farms

The Torbett family got its start in the greenhouse business when Eli Torbett Sr. started selling sweet potato slips to make a living to support his 12 children. Sweet potato slips are tiny sweet potato sprouts that are planted to grow more sweet potatoes. Their mother, Etta Fitzgerald Torbett, had died in 1925 when the youngest child - Eli "Tab" Torbett Jr. - was only four years old.

Hugh Torbett came to America in the mid-18th century and Robert Torbett came in 1734. There were several Torbett families, including Hugh, John, Robert, and Samuel. They first migrated to Pennsylvania and then moved to Sullivan County where they lived on the Cherokee Indian purchase and reared large families.

John Torbett, Eli Torbett Sr.'s great grandfather, paid taxes on Sullivan County land in 1796, according to family history.

The Torbetts were pioneers in the plant and flower growing industry of Piney Flats. Eli Torbett's descendants are still operating and managing the Torbett Greenhouses in Piney Flats. The flowers are sold locally and are transported into the surrounding southeast region. The Torbett family has always had a love for growing flowers.

Eli Anderson Torbett Sr. and his family are pictured here in Piney Flats. John Alexander Torbett's home on Carter Hill Road is pictured below. (Courtesy Janie Torbett)

An article in the July 5, 1953, issue of the Bristol Herald Courier spoke about Herbert L. Torbett, owner and operator of the Beech Springs Farm, which had nearly an acre under glass in the growing of flower and vegetable plants.

Herbert was one of 10 landowners of the Bethel community engaged in a big way in the greenhouse business. At the time, other greenhouse operators included Eli A. Torbett, Eli A. Torbett Jr., C.B. Torbett, F.J. Torbett, Carl King, Edra Allison, R.J. Alison, Leonard Allison, Leonard Osborne and R.M. Anderson.

Herbert Torbett first began to grow cut flowers, producing carnations as a hobby, the article states. A commercial florist said he would like to buy carnations from him, so he began enlarging and improving his greenhouse space. The first year he produced 1,200 carnations. In 1952, Torbett cut 160,000. He expected to produce about 250,000 carnations in 1953.

The carnations and mums were the most popular flowers at the greenhouse. They would often be used in floral designs and other general purposes.

Plants and flowers from the greenhouses, including vegetables, were taken by truck to points as far as Middlesboro Kentucky; Pulaski, Virginia; Columbia, South Carolina; and Knoxville, Tennessee. Cut flowers were sold locally to five cities: Bristol, Johnson City, Elizabethton, Kingsport, and Erwin.

Each grower participating in the farm specialized in some particular crop and thus they worked cooperatively in the sale of their products, pulling together their products, and assisting each other in the shipping.

They saved money by building their greenhouses with their own farm labor and having the cypress, a light and rot resistant wood, ripped and grooved by the nearby Wolfe Brothers furniture factory in Piney Flats. They used available local workers to put together the pipe frame greenhouse and installing the glass that had been ordered by the carload.

The weather dictated greenhouse production in Piney Flats. A Feb. 6, 1935, issue of the Johnson City Chronicle reported "Farmers of this place have been delayed this week with their plowing on account of the ground being frozen."

The article also noted that Eli Torbett was rebuilding his greenhouse in order to grow early plants.

Eli Torbett Jr., also known as Tab, was one of the millions of young Americans to be drafted during World War II. After the attack at Pearl Harbor, Tab headed to Germany and France. Once the ship docked, Tab's unit was assigned to help transport supplies to a base camp and he was part of a unit that operated a 155-millimeter howitzer, a large artillery piece which had a range of up to nine miles. Luckily, Tab left the war in Europe with no injuries, only frost-bitten feet which led to neuropathy.

Tab returned home to Sullivan County and married Peggy Penuel. They lived in Piney Flats and worked at his father Eli's sawmill and greenhouses. Later in life, Tab would open his own greenhouse, known as Johnson City Plant Farm, and operate it until a heart attack in 1991, according to an article in the Johnson City Press.

In August 2021, a Johnson City Press reporter spoke to him by phone for his 100th birthday.

"I feel good, real good right now," he said from Brookdale Senior Living, where he has resided in recent years. "I put out a garden at Brookdale. I had

Eli "Tab" Torbett Jr. served in the military. (Courtesy Janie Torbett)

an early crop of tomatoes, and I put out a second crop. It worked out real good. When the first were gone the second was coming in."

Aside from gardening at Brookdale, and enjoying the facility's various activities, Tab still goes on outings with his daughter, Kevyn Torbett, and niece, Janie Torbett--who provided many photographs and stories for this book. He also attends church at New Bethel Presbyterian Church, where he has been a lifelong member and an elder. He visited the church for a 100th birthday celebration during the summer of 2021. His wife Peggy died in 2018--she had been a secretary and executive assistant at various businesses over the years and a successful salesperson for Tupperware.

A member of the Torbett family shared health advice in the April 1906 issue of Practical Farmer. "If persons who are troubled with sore throat will bathe the throat and back of ears with cold water every time they bathe face and hands, they will surely find that they will not be troubled much with sore throat. Even use ice water," Mrs. F. Torbett said in the publication.

The homes of the Torbetts dot the landscaping of the New Bethel community. John Alexander Torbett's homeplace was located on Carter Hill Road. John (1849-1923) was the son of Hugh and Elizabeth Torbett. He served with the 60th Tennessee Infantry and the 1st Special Battalion during the Civil War. He constructed his log house in the early 19th century. The home features 24-inch logs which can now be seen from the basement. The house is now covered in siding and still stands. Another Torbett home is located in the 800 block of Pickens Bridge Road. The farmhouse features a central hall plan, meaning a hall stretches across the home and rooms can be found on both sides of the corridor.

Like many families in the region, the Torbett family has often held reunions over the years. The family began gathering in 1928. The fifth reunion was held at the home of Clifford Torbett on Aug. 7, 1932. The sixth reunion was then held in the grove of the home of D.W. Oliver and was hosted by Clifford Torbett. The Bristol Herald Courier reported that more than 150 people attended the event, which included a "splendid talk" by the Reverend E. Roy Gentry. The New Bethel and Edgefield church choirs rendered several musical selections during the reunion.

Information on the Torbett family was provided by Janie Torbett and also gleaned from local newspaper articles.

The Torbett family operated a cheese factory in this structure along Pickens Bridge Road. It has since been converted into a home. It is located near the family's nurseries. (Courtesy Janie Torbett)

Cheese factories

Several cheese factories once operated in rural Piney Flats, providing extra income for local farmers and affordable dairy products for households across the region. The cheese factories in the community operated during the early 20th century and were organized as cooperatives between farmers and other shareholders. One, the Weaver Branch Cheese Factory, was considered the most successful operation in Tennessee.

In the early days of the U.S., dairy farms were relatively small and remotely located. They had challenges that were best resolved with cooperative agreements. Agricultural cooperatives sprang up spontaneously across rural America, formed by groups of farmers seeking solutions to common problems, such as transportation and marketing, according to a history of dairy cooperatives by the U.S. Department of Agriculture. The groups drew upon cooperative traditions that immigrant dairy farmers had brought with them from Europe. Milk from several farms was pooled in one location, either by hauling milk or cream in cans or by taking cows to the factory to be milked. Milk was then made into cheese or butter. A portion of the net proceeds was then returned to the farmers depending on the amount of milk each provided.

The first reported cooperative cheese factories were established in the U.S. in the mid-1800s. The creameries grew slowly until mechanical cream separators were introduced around 1890, the USDA history states. By the 1920s, there were cooperative dairy associations in all but six states.

Rural cheese manufacturing arrived in the Piney Flats area in 1916-1917 thanks to Garrett N. Tobey of the University of Tennessee Agricultural Extensions Service. Tobey, born in New York in 1879, moved to Knoxville, Tennessee, in 1916 to join the agricultural office.

"He came here to be a cheese specialist," according to his obituary published in the Knoxville Journal.

One year later, the first cheese factory in Tennessee was created in the Weaver Branch section of Piney Flats.

Tobey, who died in 1938, gave technical advice and assistance in founding the factory. "UT sure helped this neighborhood out when they sent Mr. Tobey here," said W.C. Webb of the factory's leadership.

Gabe W. Oliver donated the land for the factory, and the deed stipulated the land belonged to the stockholders as long as the factory operated, according to Gene Morrell. When the business ceased to operate, the land returned to the Oliver heirs, the deed states.

Morrell said early directors of the cooperative included local farmers Brack Cross, Will Webb, John Webb, Sam Hart, G.W. Jones, Walter Weaver, and Will Cross, who also served as the first president and chief salesman for the cheese products. The directors were required to purchase stock in the company which had shares at $25 and the stock drew eight percent dividends at one time, according to Morrell, who quoted Virginia Hancher. Hancher, a prominent 20th century educator and historian in Sullivan County, lived near the cheese factory.

Will J. Cross maintained a sales route for the cheese in Johnson City, Kingsport, Jonesborough, Erwin, and Abingdon and Saltville in Virginia. Cross used a hack with horses to transport the cheese along the road during the early years. He later hauled the cheese in a truck and hired local men to drive.

Local Piney Flats farmers delivered the milk to the factory. They were paid according to the percentage of butter fat the milk contained. Morrell said round blocks of cheese made at the factory came in different sizes, and the cheese was aged in a separate room at the factory.

Cheese produced at the factory was entered in fairs throughout the area, and at one time the makers won many ribbons.

The Feb. 1, 1927, issue of the Bristol News Bulletin said: "Cheese men to hold meet." The shareholders of the Weaver Branch Cooperative Cheese Factory were preparing to meet to discuss business.

At the time, the factory annually produced from $16,000 to $20,000 worth of cheese and other dairy products. The annual meeting held at the factory was regarded as extremely important by the residents and others interested in cheese manufacturing, according to Sullivan County Agricultural Agent H.P. Bird.

According to reports, stockholders continued to realize dividends up until about 1950 despite the fact that the factory closed in 1942. After the factory closed, farmers banded together and sold their milk and products through a local dairy in cooperation with the contract for the factory.

By 1954, the newspaper reported that new officers were going to reopen the factory, renovate the building, and the equipment was sent to Richmond, Virginia, for refining. No records show that it reopened, and the building continued to deteriorate.

The factory at Weaver Branch wasn't the only one to produce cheese in Piney Flats. Another one, known as New Bethel Cheese, operated for several years along Pickens Bridge Road. Several families, including the Torbett and Anderson families, operated the factory in a building that has since been transformed into a private residence.

Rotha Torbett Fagans and her husband Charlie ran the family cheese factory, according to a written history provided by the Torbetts. It was owned by Eli Torbett, Rotha's brother. The cheese factory operated during the 1920s, around the same time as the Weaver Branch factory. It also received assistance from Tobey, the cheese specialist from Knoxville. There were two upright broilers at the Torbett facility that would heat the coils that processed milk to churn and produce the cheese. The whey, a liquid byproduct of cheese production, was then used to feed the hogs.

In 1927, the New Bethel Cheese factory was listed for sale in the Johnson City Staff-News. It listed one six horsepower boiler and full equipment for making cheese. After it closed, the factory became the home of Gene and Monta Torbett Hale. Monta was Eli Torbett's daughter.

The Warren family

Edmond Warren, the oldest son of John Warren, was born about 1738 and is considered the founding member of the Warren family of Tennessee, according to information provided by Janie Torbett. Edmond Warren married and lived in Pennsylvania. He also served during the Revolutionary War, helping drive General George Cornwallis out of North Carolina and he fought at the Battle at Kings Mountain in South Carolina.

Edmond returned to Pennsylvania, but then moved to the Appalachian Mountain region. He settled along the Holston River, about five miles south of Bristol. He obtained a land grant of about 400 acres on Dec. 15, 1794, and he erected a hand-hewn log house, which was known as the original Warren house.

Edmond and his wife had three sons, including Michael, who also had three children. One of Michael's children, Eli Warren, born in 1805, bought a farm of about 160 acres at the head of Weaver Branch, two miles north of Piney Flats. He built a house in 1842, which has been described as 50 feet long and 25 feet wide, two stories high, constructed of hand-hewn logs, according to Torbett's information.

Eli and his wife had three children at the home. His son William Edmond Warren assumed the responsibilities as head of household at the age of 16. The Warren boys helped on the farm, cleaning stables. Several of the older boys left home early to work for other farmers and soon were married. The old Warren homestead is no longer standing.

In 1886, William Warren purchased land on the north side of the Watauga River, and a few years later acquired a farm on the south side, making a total of 600 acres. He purchased the first mowing machine in the community about 1880, and two years later, he bought the first reaper, according to information provided by Torbett.

The King family

The King family—a prominent Piney Flats family—originally emigrated from England to the United States in the mid-17th century. They arrived in Massachusetts looking for a new life and success that enticed many others before them to head to the colonies.

In 1782, Edward King Sr. (1720-1790) was issued a large land grant of about 640 acres in Piney Flats in what was then Washington County, North Carolina, according to information provide by Janie Torbett. A veteran of the Revolutionary War, King is listed in Captain Jacob van Braam's company in William Armstrong Crozier's Virginia Militia. He was awarded 100 acres of land for services at the Battle of the Meadows and Fort Necessity, Pennsylvania, where George Washington was placed in his first command, according to the Century Farms Program at the Center for Historic Preservation at Middle Tennessee State University.

Edward King is considered to be the primary ancestor of the family of Kings that lived in Piney Flats and later Bristol. He moved to the area about 11 years after William Bean settled down at nearby Boones Creek. The King farm on Warren Drive in Piney Flats is now designated a Tennessee Pioneer Century Farm.

Married to Elizabeth Nichols (1728-1808), the couple had one son, John King, who was born in 1758. Edward and Elizabeth were charter members at the New Bethel Presbyterian Church, which Rev. Doak organized in 1782.

After his father's death, John King acquired the farm. John King fathered 10 children. Hay, corn, wheat, cattle, and horses were among the farm products at the King Farm.

"John was a leading citizen of the Fork Settlement and was an important factor in establishing civilization and Christianity in this beautiful county," the family told the Pioneer Century Farms program.

John King's son, Isaac King, and grandson, Edward Rutledge King, later came into possession of the farm. Edward King was in charge of shelling corn and loading a barge at nearby Allison's Mill for the river journey to Knoxville during the Civil War, the family said.

More recently, the historic farm has been owned by Steven Edward King and his wife Teresa Lynn, according to the Pioneer Century Farms program. The farm currently occupies more than 200 acres and includes a beef and dairy cattle operation. They also have Tennessee walking horses, tobacco, hay, and grains.

While many dairy farms have downsized or ceased operation, King Farm continues to milk 180 cows and produces an average of 20,000 pounds of milk per cow each year.

The King house, a brick structure, was constructed in 1879. There are also several barns and outbuildings dating from the late 19th century and early 20th century.

The Warrens and Kings are two of the oldest families residing in the New Bethel community Piney Flats. Their ancestors have farmed the soil for more than 200 years. The New Bethel Church and Edgefield Church, and graveyards, feature six or seven generations, and at least 60 names connected to those families

The King Brothers

Another arm of the King family of Piney Flats includes five brothers that went on to become successful citizens of nearby Bristol in the late 19th century and early 20th century. The brothers--Henry Preston King (1862-1957), Landon Clayton King (1871-1954), Edward Washington King (1852-1945), Rutledge King (1866-1957), and Anson King (1860-1954) --grew up during the Civil War era in rural Piney Flats. They grew up with another brother, Justin, who died at a young age, and six sisters. Their parents, William and Emma Hodge King, were not wealthy. All of the children attended rural public schools in Sullivan County, primarily in the New Bethel community, where they were raised.

Henry Preston King, Edward Washington King, and Landon Clayton King-- better known by their first two initials H.P., E.W., and L.C.--all worked for a period of time in their uncle James King's store in the Rocky Springs community. James King operated White's Store, a successful rural general store and a post office. During his time at the store, H.P. acted as station manager and postmaster, in addition to his duties as salesman.

H.P. later went on into business for himself in Johnson City, where he founded a retail store and in 1889, he moved to Bristol. There, he established the H.P. King Co., which became one of the most successful mercantile organizations in the Appalachian Mountain region. It was located on State Street between Sixth and Seventh streets.

His brother E.W., later a successful businessman in Bristol, often told stories of his time in Piney Flats. He helped pay his school tuition by doing chores, sweeping, and building fires. He then worked for eight years at his uncle's store. Out of his salary, he saved $1,000 and in 1878 came to Bristol to open a small retail business on State Street.

In 1882, E.W. built a two-story structure on State Street which housed his dry goods company until 1893 when he constructed a new and larger building. He took advantage of the shortage of ready cash after the economic panic of 1898 to expand his company which he called the E.W. King and Company. The company became extremely successful as the first exclusively wholesale business between Knoxville, Tennessee, and Roanoke, Virginia.

E.W. also served more than fifty years as a member of the board of trustees of King College, a local Presbyterian school, which conferred an honorary degree upon him several years before his death. He was made a lifelong board member. E.W. and his wife were prominent members of First Presbyterian Church in Bristol. The college is named after the Rev. James King family, different than the King brothers.

Aside from being chairman of the board of the E.W. King Company, he served many years as president of the First National Bank and later as vice president and chairman of the bank's board, according to his obituary.

E.W. also formed the King Brothers Shoe Company in 1901 with his brother Anson King. According to news accounts, the shoe company grew by the mid-20th century to become one of the four largest wholesale shoe distributors in the nation.

At the age of 16, L.C. joined his brother E.W.'s wholesale dry goods business and worked there as a salesman for 25 years before deciding to start his own business, a clothing company. The L.C. King Manufacturing Co. continues to operate out of a factory in downtown Bristol.

"An avid huntsman of quail and rabbit, he loved the art of raising and training the pointer breed of hunting dog," according to a company history about L.C. "He admired their qualities, especially those champion dogs who competed in tournaments. It is clear that the bond between dog, man, and gun was strong throughout his life. When it came time to name his clothing line, he decided to consider the admirable characteristics of the dogs a noble metaphor for the values of a company and the products he would make, as well as something that would translate in the marketplace to consumers."

White's Store

The two-story White's Store is an historic landmark in the Rocky Springs section of Piney Flats. This former business, which today sits along a cove of Boone Lake, served as a postal station and general store for the rural community. It was originally constructed in 1881 and still features a 20-foot

The White's Store is located in the Rocky Springs community of Piney Flats. It previously housed a Post Office. (Courtesy Janie Torbett)

by 50-foot store, restored by recent owners. It maintains its integrity without changing the brick walls or the two rows of glass front cabinets, according to a real estate listing from 2021. There are large 10-foot tall original doors at the front of the building along with a large front porch. A large original pot-bellied stove sits in the middle of the store. From the first floor, guests can climb the staircase to a five-foot-wide balcony on three sides of the store.

The store lasted through the earlier 20th century and employed members of the King family, including future businessmen E.W. King and H.P. King. Both Kings helped manage the store, which was owned by James King. It was later known as Burkie's Store and Walter Phillips' Store. When a post office operated in the building the surrounding community was known by the postal service as White Station.

White's Store was often used as a geographic location in newspapers during the 19th and early 20th century.

Col. Nathan Gregg

Nathan Gregg (1835-1894) was one of the most prominent men in East Tennessee during the 19th century. He resided with his wife in the Rocky Springs section of Piney Flats. He spent most of his life in the public eye, having served as a local sheriff and in the Tennessee legislature.

During the war, Gregg fought as a Confederate soldier, commanding the 60th Tennessee Mounted Infantry Regiment. The regiment was organized in 1862, according to the National Park Service. They mustered into Confederate service on Nov. 7, 1862. Most of the regiment was either captured at the Big Black River Bridge or at Vicksburg. The men served the remainder of the war in Vaughn's Brigade and skirmished in East Tennessee and Western Virginia. They disbanded during the spring of 1865. It was during his military service that he received a wound, which was the primary cause of his death later in life. Upon returning home, Gregg served three terms as sheriff of Sullivan County from 1870 to 1876. He also served three terms in the state legislature from 1876 to 1882. He was appointed pension agent during the administration of President Grover Cleveland.

Gregg and his wife, Catherine Gregg, were great benefactors of educational and religious projects in their hometown. The couple had no children, and they bequeathed his estate to the Bertha King Memorial Presbyterian Church in Rocky Springs and to a niece, Jannett Gregg. They are buried at New Bethel Church.

Rocky Springs

The Bertha King Memorial Presbyterian Church was built at Rocky Springs in 1905. According to Col. Nathan Gregg's will, E.W. King, the executor, sold for $1 to the trustees of the Bertha King Memorial Presbyterian Church one acre of land for use as the site of the church and a place of public worship.

Before moving to Bristol, King married Alice Millard on Oct. 10, 1877. She was a daughter of George and Elzira Millard who were near neighbors in Piney Flats. Two years later, on Aug. 30, 1879, the first child of E.W. and Alice King was born, according to late Bristol historian and author Bud Phillips. She was a beautiful girl they named Bertha. She was their pride and

The Presbyterian church at Rocky Springs is one of the oldest in Sullivan County. It was founded in the 1800s. The brick church with a large belfry and bell is pictured here. It is located on Rocky Springs Road near Alison Road in Piney Flats. (Photo by author)

joy, becoming more beautiful as she grew older. She was of a sweet cheerful disposition, endearing herself to all who knew her. Early in school, she proved herself to be a budding intellectual. Under the tutelage of a local music teacher, Bertha learned to play the piano. Her father bought her a piano for home practice. She also developed a beautiful singing voice for one so young, Phillips wrote in an article in the Bristol Herald Courier.

Then, Bertha came down with a disease, one for which there was no cure at the time, Phillips said. She died Oct. 3, 1889, a little over a month past her 10th birthday. She was buried in historic East Hill Cemetery in Bristol.

This singing group attended the Presbyterian church in Rocky Springs. (Courtesy Janie Torbett)

Her great uncle, Col. Gregg made provision in his will for a Presbyterian church to be erected in Piney Flats that would be a memorial to this deceased Bertha King, Phillips said. In 1906, a fine brick church with very beautiful stained-glass windows was erected at what is now 3297 Rocky Springs Road in Piney Flats. The bricks used to construct the church were handmade on the site. The stained-glass windows were so beautiful that the church has even been offered $30,000 but will not sell.

The building at Rocky Springs was a community church which was composed of Methodists, Baptists, and Presbyterian. A clause in the deed permitted any denomination to use the building when not in use by the congregation regularly worshiping there.

Rocky Springs School is now abandoned and is missing its bell. The schoolhouse is located along Rocky Springs Road in Piney Flats. (Photo by author)

Bertha King Memorial Presbyterian Church is now known as Rocky Springs Baptist Church. Early members included J.W. Boring, J.R. Clay, B.H. McKamey, J.W. Jeter, E.J. Burkey, John Sanders, Guilford Torbett, H.D. McCleland, Watson Anderson, E.S. Blalock, William Collins, and William Poe. The original trustees for the church were Burkey, E.R. King, J.F. Gross, and Bertha's father, E.W. King.

An old schoolhouse stands near the Rocky Springs Baptist Church. According to Sullivan County News, Nathan Gregg deeded one-half acre in 1884 for the establishment of a public free school. A local resident told the newspaper that this was the site of Rocky Springs School. The school operated during the first half of the 20th century. The white sided building with an empty belfry remains vacant.

Enterprise

The community of Enterprise, a rural section of Piney Flats along Boone Lake about five miles from the village, was once known as Jeter Mill. The Jeter family had operated a mill on the Holston River near the old Droke farm. George and Cora Jeter lived in the Enterprise community their entire

118

lives. Now buried at the Droke Cemetery, George Jeter owned and operated the mill. It also served as a mail pick-up station for Enterprise, according to Families and History of Sullivan County, Tennessee Volume One. A flood later destroyed the mill.

Enterprise Road now stretches across the rolling hills. It was once a very rocky, winding road. An historic church now sits at the center of Enterprise.

The Enterprise School and Church were built on a rocky slope when an even older school, known as DeVault School, burned. William B. and Elizabeth Cross Millhorn provided land in 1894 for the school and church. DeVault School, a log building, had been built during the Civil War. Funds from DeVault School were used to build Enterprise School. Millhorn and others in the community helped build the one-room school. R.B. Cross was the school's first teacher. A school operated at Enterprise until 1948.

A Dutch meeting house was also located in the Enterprise community.

In the early days, Enterprise Church served all denominations. In the 1950s, the church became Methodist and new rooms were built, according to Families and History of Sullivan County, Tennessee Volume One. In 1963, a brick building was constructed adjoining the old church, which was also bricked and remodeled, the book states.

Early family names on the Enterprise Church roll include Cross, Smith, Morrell, Millhorn, DeVault, Crussell, Phillips, Houston, Hicks, Malone, Lindamood, Warren, Massengill, Deakins, Jeter, McHenry, Shepard, Oliver, Combs, Droke, and Morris, the book states.

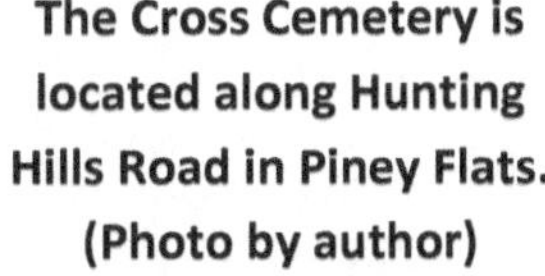

The Cross Cemetery is located along Hunting Hills Road in Piney Flats. (Photo by author)

The Cross family, a pioneer Sullivan County family, has attended Enterprise United Methodist Church. The large family, which operated several businesses and owned large farms, hosted reunions annually at the church. In 1949, more than 200 people attended the Cross family reunion, according to the Bristol Herald Courier. Pioneer Elijah Cross I was a Revolutionary War soldier.

Enterprise Road crosses Boone Lake at the Rainbow Bridge. There were four cemeteries near the bridge. Lindamood Cemetery was located at the end of the bridge, where slaves are said to have been buried. Droke Cemetery was located on the Droke farm, Smith Cemetery was located of Rice Cross Road and Gross Cemetery was located on the Warren farm. The Warren farm was also the site of the Gross Store and a post office. The Gross store was the mustering site for local military units during the Civil War. A post office also once operated at the R.B. Cross home. Another store, owned by the Woods family, operated on the Morrell farm. Howard Phillips Cash operated a market in Enterprise in the 1950s.

Information on the Enterprise community was gleaned from newspaper articles, particularly from Gene Morrell of the Sullivan County News, who wrote a regular column on county history.

Poplar Ridge
This beautiful vista can be found in the Poplar Ridge section of Piney Flats.
The Appalachian Mountains can be seen in the background.
(Photo by Dalena Adams)

Poplar Ridge Christian Church was founded in the early 1800s and is located just off Poplar Ridge Road. (Photo by author)

Poplar Ridge

The Poplar Ridge Christian Church, pictured above, in Piney Flats is one of the region's oldest congregations. It was founded in the early 19th Century. Originally, it was known as the Forks Church, and was established in 1842, according to Families and History of Sullivan County, Tennessee Volume One. The original church had 43 members, the book states. By 1846, the church had assumed the name Poplar Ridge Christian Church. At that time, it had 73 members.

According to Sullivan County records, in July 1904, the Smith family donated land to the elders of Poplar Ridge Church. The land was to be used as church land and as a location to develop a cemetery. Four years later, the Brown family sold two acres to the board of education and trustees of Poplar Ridge Church. The land was to be used for the church and a school playground.

The old Poplar Ridge School, which burned down, originally had two potbellied stoves and the students were responsible for supplying wood for those stoves. Students would also retrieve water from a nearby well.

A new church as constructed in 1949 and remodeled in 1959. A new sanctuary was later built in 1990 and seated more than 400 people. In 1964, Poplar Ridge Christian Church dedicated a new parsonage. Work on the home was completed by church members. The parsonage had three bedrooms, two bathrooms, a kitchen, living room with a stone fireplace, and there was a family room in the basement.

Poplar Ridge was the site of a 1969 reunion for two local brothers who hadn't seen each other for 51 years, according to an article in the Johnson City Press. The brothers, Henry Shepherd, of Tacoma, Washington, and Bill Shepherd, of Elizabethton, Tennessee, met with three other brothers and three sisters to celebrate the occasion. Henry, the oldest of the family, left their Poplar Grove home at the age of 17.

"I worked for construction companies and did some railroad work before joining the Army in 1915," he said.

Henry remained in the Army for more than 30 years and retired in 1952. Their parents, Robert and Mary Ellen, farmed in the Poplar Ridge area most of their lives. Bill was the youngest of the siblings and lived in the area all his life, having worked in Elizabethton at a loan company.

Roy Broyles works in the field.
(Courtesy Piney Flats Historical Society)

Houston Farm

The historic Houston Farm is located in the Hunting Hills section of Piney Flats. It was founded around 1780 and is designated as a Century Farm by the state of Tennessee, having been owned by six generations of one family. The farm is part of an original land grant from North Carolina for service in the Revolutionary War and has been farmed continuously by Cole family descendants. The present farm, located off Hunting Hills Road, was inhabited around 1896 by Mary Isabelle Cole and her husband, Charlie Deakins, who built the three-story brick home. Their daughter, Virginia "Pet" and

Houston Farm in Piney Flats.
(Photos by author)

husband J.W. Houston, a descendent of Sam Houston, farmed the property until it was owned by their daughter and son-in-law, Mary Frances Houston and Audra Malone.

Charlie Houston, son of "Pet" and J.W. Houston, served Sullivan County for 36 years as a magistrate, member of the county court, chairman of the Sullivan County State Election Commission, and president of the state of Tennessee Election Commission.

The more than 100-acre farm features the 2,100 square foot brick home that was built in 1901. The bricks were made near the farm. There are also two barn cribs and a loft barn that were constructed in the early 1930s. The original farmhouse is no longer in use and a new farmhouse was built in 2000.

Deer Lick

The Deer Lick community of Piney Flats is home to the Union Church, which was founded in the late 19th century. A school, founded after the Civil War, was also established in Deer Lick. It was destroyed by fire in 1935. Nearby, the Geisler family operated a store and owned hundreds of acres of land. The family continues to live and work in the Deer Lick community.

The Deer Lick Union Church is one of the oldest churches in Piney Flats. It is located off Deer Lick Road, which is near the Haw Ridge area. (Photo by author)

St. Paul Methodist Church

The St. Paul Methodist Church on Alison Road in Piney Flats was originally built in 1950. Its congregation was established in 1892, according to the church. Morrell said the congregation existed as early as 1878. The church originally met in the old Rocky Springs School building, and later in the second schoolhouse. The congregation held services in the school until 1905, when it met at the Bertha King Memorial Presbyterian Church. The Methodists utilized the building when the Presbyterian congregation was not holding services.

By 1949, the local Methodist circuit divided, and St. Paul and others formed the Piney Flats Methodist Church. In 1951, the congregation began construction of St. Paul Methodist when the Burdine family donated one acre of land for the church site.

The church was officially dedicated in December of 1958 on the sixth anniversary of its opening service in 1952. A Methodist church could not be dedicated until it was debt free, according to the Sullivan County News.

Fairview

Fairview is located on the opposite side of Boone Lake near Blountville but is part of Piney Flats. Hulls Chapel, one of the oldest Methodist churches in Sullivan County, is located along DeVault Bridge Road. The historic Holston Grove Lutheran Church, located along Sugar Hollow Road, was organized in 1903, according to local historian Shelia Steele Hunt. It was organized in 1903, and was on the roll of the local synod, or assembly, until 1959. Steele-Hunt said its church members were among the old South Fork Settlement of early pioneers.

An explosion damaged Earl Trivette's gas station in Piney Flats in the 1940s. (Courtesy Janie Torbett)

Many new friends toured Piney Flats East Tennessee Junior Cycling Omnium bicycle race that started in the village. (Courtesy Piney Flats Historical Society)

CHAPTER SEVEN

Twentieth Century

During the early 1900s, local society columns in the Tri-Cities often shared news about families and friends visiting Spurgeon Island for parties, picnics, and camping. It was a spot for youthful scouts to camp and learn about the outdoors. Many locals also referred the island, located near the confluence of the Watauga and Holston rivers, as a "lovers lane" type destination, a place for young couples to enjoy an evening alone.

In late 1949 and early 1950, residents in the Tri-Cities began hearing about the Tennessee Valley Authority's plan to construct two dams as part of the Upper Holston Project. The federal agency--tasked with flood control and power production, had already been working on the construction of dams at Watauga and South Holston. The TVA outlined the next step in the orderly development of the water resources of the Tennessee Valley, particularly the construction of Boone and Fort Patrick Henry projects.

The two projects were to be built at Spurgeon Island and Wexler Bend. The Holston River Power Company had long sought to construct dams similar to those that the Tennessee Valley Authority built. In the 1920s, the power company surveyed the river basin with plans to build four dams and identified the present Boone site (the company called it the "Bachman Ford" site). It should be noted that one dam, Wilbur Dam, was constructed in Carter County in 1912. It is below the Watauga Dam.

In the early 1930s, the TVA--which came about as part of President Franklin D. Roosevelt's New Deal--assumed oversight of flood control operations in the Tennessee River watershed, which includes the Watauga and Holston rivers. Much of the region was affected by poverty before and during the Great Depression. The region had the resources, but development, production, and consumption were limited. Economic development depended on good transportation, adequate flood control, and a supply of affordable electricity.

In 1933, the TVA built a dam on the Clinch River. The Norris Dam was completed in 1936 and became the TVA's first operating dam. Nine additional dams were constructed in the 1930s and four in the 1940s. The dams of Northeast Tennessee were then constructed in the 1950s as America returned to peacetime following World War II.

The agency suggested the Boone site as a potential dam location. As work progressed on the Watauga and South Holston dams, the TVA looked at the next logical step in development of the watershed. The project's primary purpose was to provide flood control in the region, especially in the industrial city of Kingsport, which suffered from major flood damage in 1901 and 1940.

Described in the fall of 1949 in the TVA's program for fiscal year 1951, the projects were submitted to the federal Bureau of Budget. The plans were presented to begin construction on Boone Dam, to be constructed at Spurgeon Island, in 1951 and for work preparation to begin at Wexler Bend on the Fort Patrick Henry project in 1952.

The Tennessee Valley Authority provided these photographs of the Boone Dam project. (Photos courtesy Tennessee Valley Authority)

Hundreds of people worked to build the Boone Dam in Piney Flats.
(Photos courtesy Tennessee Valley Authority)

The plans were designed to allow workers and equipment to move from project to project.

The Bureau of Budget approved the plans, and they became part of the President Harry S. Truman's budget for fiscal year 1951. They were sent to congress in January 1950, according to a TVA report on the projects.

On Sept. 6, 1950, Truman signed and approved appropriations for the Boone Dam and Fort Patrick Henry Dam projects.

Boone Dam, named for frontiersman Daniel Boone, was expected to tie into the face of Spurgeon's knob, which was just across the river from the Piney Flats home of R.L. Milhorn and a few yards upstream from Spurgeon's Island. Gigantic in proportions, and with beautiful super-structure, the dam was planned to reach almost half-way up the face of the knob and would extend back through Milhorn's yard to a point about 200 feet behind his house, according to the TVA report.

Boone Dam is a hydroelectric and flood control dam. It cost the federal government $27,191,574. Boone Reservoir, the lake created by Boone Dam, covers about 5,420 acres. When the dam closed, water inundated farmland

Dozens of gravesites were relocated due to the Boone Dam construction project, include those at this cemetery off Haw Ridge Road in Piney Flats. (Photo by author)

across Sullivan and Washington counties, especially in the Piney Flats area. Land and land rights were acquired amounting to about 5,160 acres, which required the moving of 152 families, according to TVA records. About 1,363 acres of timber was also cleared. In addition, highways, roads, and streets were also constructed, totaling about 18 miles, including 1.4 miles of highways, 16.3 miles of county roads, and .2 miles of city streets in Bluff City. Three bridges were also constructed across the reservoir. About 21 miles of utility lines were constructed or moved, and 104 graves were removed and relocated.

When the Tennessee Valley Authority constructed Boone Dam, some work was required on the Pickens Bridge, Rainbow Bridge, and DeVault Bridge. (Photo by author)

No state highways were relocated, but extensive work was done on U.S. Highway 11E at its bridges over the Watauga and South Holston rivers. Piney Flats, which is dependent on its bridge and road system to surrounding communities, was also affected by work on Pickens Bridge, DeVault Bridge, and Rainbow Bridge.

The original Rainbow Bridge on Enterprise Road was constructed in the 1920s, according to the *Sullivan County News.* The bridge was a local landmark and was a reference point for residents. The newspaper said it was constructed of sand, cement, and native stones, and the bridge had a rainbow shape, hence its name. A contractor from Knoxville constructed the bridge using manpower and horsepower. Cement was mixed by hand, loaded into wheelbarrows, and poured into molds. Several people who worked on the old bridge lived in tents near the site, the newspaper said.

After the original bridge was demolished, the new bridge was constructed nearby.

The book Mountain Memories also discusses an island that was submerged nearby due to the lake. There was evidence that it was inhabited by Native Americans, locals said. Numerous native arrowheads and hatchet heads could be found on the island.

The old Rainbow Bridge was replaced along with the DeVault Bridge and Pickens Bridge, according to the TVA report. The TVA conducted studies on the bridges to determine whether one could be eliminated, but because of the resulting increase in travel distances no plan could be discovered which was acceptable to officials in Washington and Sullivan counties. As a result of the decision to replace the three bridges at their current sites, the primary county road system was basically preserved and the county road relocation was confined to raising or relocating small sections of the road to prevent isolation of small communities or even individuals where economically feasible, according to the report.

Work on Pickens Bridge even received honorable mention for the class III award in the Prize Bridge Competition conducted by the American Institute of Steel Construction for 1952.

Local bridge builders won an award for their work on Pickens Bridge in 1952. (Photo by author)

This view of Boone Lake can be seen off Haw Ridge Road in Piney Flats. The lake provides visitors and residents with many panoramic views. (Photo by author)

Some other bridges, including Cobb Creek Bridge, Muddy Creek Bridge, and Beaver Creek Bridge, also required work.

Records show Boone Dam's construction resulted in the acquisition of 698 tracts of land. About 96.7% of private owners voluntarily conveyed property to the government while 2.3% were condemned due to property owners refusing to sell. Another one percent was condemned to clear defective titles. Seven businesses moved. One school and one church were relocated. A total of 42 homes and other buildings were moved intact.

The government conducted reconnaissance to determine the number of cemeteries and gravesites in the reservoir and its immediate vicinity. It was found that 11 cemeteries in the area would not be affected and two which would have been isolated were served by new roads constructed by TVA.

Nine cemeteries were flooded by the new reservoir, and one was rendered inaccessible by the reservoir. They contained a total of 234 graves.

Surviving relatives authorized the relocation of 104 graves and they were moved to 10 reinternment cemeteries, according to the TVA report. Ninety-two monuments and 87 footstones were moved. In addition, a large masonry memorial monument was dismantled and rebuilt on a new location above the reservoir. The monument belonged to the Daughters of the American Revolution and marked the site of a cabin built by William Bean.

The Goodman Cemetery is one of the graveyards moved during construction. Sixty-three graves were removed, and seven graves remained. The report states that 45 were reinterred in the new Goodman Cemetery, which is located in the Haw Ridge Road area of Piney Flats. Four were moved to Glenwood Cemetery, four to New Bethel Cemetery, one to Sanders Cemetery and two to Monte Vista Cemetery in Johnson City.

Another cemetery, Galloway Duncan Cemetery, had 11 graves that were established before the Civil War. The cemetery is now under the lake, according to the TVA. Other affected graveyards include Hall Cemetery and Hilton Cemetery.

Boone Dam was completed, and its gates closed December 16, 1952. The dam's first generator went online March 16, 1953, its second generator went online June 12, 1953, and the third went online September 3, 1953, according to the TVA.

The reservoir, with about 168 miles of shoreline, is a V-shape waterway. It extends for 17 miles up the South Holston River, all the way to Bluff City, and up the Watauga River for about 15 miles. Boone Dam is about 31 miles downstream from South Holston Dam and 10 miles upstream from Fort Patrick Henry Dam. In a typical year, the reservoir fluctuates by about 20 feet, as the TVA lowers the water each winter.

The dam and associated infrastructure were listed on the National Register of Historic Places in 2017. The Watauga, South Holston, and Fort Patrick Henry dams are also listed on the national register. Boone Lake has a visitor building overlooking the reservoir. One unique decorative feature at the visitor center is an original mural painted by Kingsport-based TVA staff artist Robert Birdwell.

Numerous permanent homes and summer cabins were constructed on privately owned shorelands before the lake was opened to fishing, according to the TVA report. One private yacht club was established during the first year of reservoir impoundment. Fifteen boat docks were established or had been approved when the lake was opened to fishing during the second spring of impoundment.

The automobile has also played a major part in Piney Flats' history in the 20th century, including the development of the local road system and the proposal to build America's next great motor speedway.

During the early 20th century, America's preferred mode of transportation began to change from the train to the automobile. Following the introduction to Henry Ford's Model T in 1908, roads began to be constructed across the United States. By the 1920s, U.S. Highway 11E was constructed from Strawberry Plains, just east of Knoxville, to Bristol, Virginia.

Much of the work on the highway in the 1920s was done by mules pulling graders and scrapers. Many of the construction workers lived in tent camps along the route. One camp was located near Ordway Hill in the Avoca community of Bristol. Corrals for the mules were located near the camps. Other camps were also established near Piney Flats.

Room and board was also provided to many of the highway workers by several homeowners in Piney Flats.

Gene Morrell, a former columnist at the Sullivan County News, said Jess Cross of Piney Flats, and Raymond "Shorty" Morrell and Barnes Morrell, both of Bluff City, helped construct the highway. Morrell wrote "Mountain Memories," which shared stories from Piney Flats and other Sullivan County communities, for the newspaper.

The route of the popular highway, also known as the Bristol-Johnson City Highway, went through the historic village of Piney Flats. It followed the route that Austin Springs Road and Main Street currently takes through the community. Stores, gas stations, and other businesses opened along the route, including in Piney Flats.

In 1932, however, the highway was rerouted so that it passed about three-quarters of a mile to the northwest of Piney Flats. After the highway moved away from the village, there was no longer any attraction for new commercial development.

Highway 11E eventually became a divided four-lane highway through Piney Flats. In recent years, substantial modern retail development has taken place along both sides of the highway. The growth also led to annexation from nearby Johnson City and Bluff City.

Did you know Bristol Motor Speedway was originally planned for Piney Flats? (Courtesy National Archives)

Bristol Motor Speedway

Larry Carrier built more than 100 fine homes in the Bristol area in the 1950s. He developed new residential districts, making available the top in quality at the bottom in cost. In 1959, he stepped into a new field: entertainment. He built Larry's Lanes, the most modern and comfort conditioned bowling alley in the country.

Carrier was also interested in racing. He visited several major racetracks around the country, understanding how to develop the perfect speedway. He formulated in his fertile mind an ideal track. More than a half century later, that track is now a reality. Originally sketched on brown paper bags, napkins and the back of envelopes, Carrier and his friends Carl Moore and R.G. Pope created what is today known as Bristol Motor Speedway, one of the nation's most popular and successful racetracks.

In 1960, Moore had just attended a football game at the University of Tennessee in Knoxville and was settling into his hotel room when the telephone rang. Carrier was on the line and obviously excited.

"Larry called and said you've got to come over here. You've got to see all these people buying tickets for a stock car race. I think it might be a good venture," Moore told McGee. "So I went to Charlotte the next day and we saw that race."

The two men were among a Sunday crowd officially listed as more than 29,000, jammed into the speedway to watch a race sanctioned by the National Association of Stock Car Automobile Racing. The Florida-based organization was in its second decade and the Charlotte track was one of two new facilities to open in 1960.

In the end, the pair decided they wanted to build a racetrack, but only if they could secure dates on NASCAR's schedule. During a meeting with Bill France in Florida, the two were asked what two dates they would be interested in, McGee wrote. They chose July 30 and Oct. 28, 1961, giving them a tight deadline to build a racetrack and sell tickets.

In Tennessee, Carrier and Moore developed plans, creating an oval track nearly a mile in length, shorter than Charlotte but larger than many others. They also visited tracks at Martinsville and the former Asheville-Weaverville Speedway.

The businessmen wanted to build in Sullivan County on property in Piney Flats, about seven miles from where it was ultimately constructed. The men had plans to develop a speedway at the current sites of the Gillfield, Dogwood Park and Willow Creek subdivisions north of Alison Road and west of U.S. Highway 11E. Carrier's family already owned land in the area, according to deed records, and his father, Hugh Carrier, was a local real estate agent. He found some rolling acreage and took an option to purchase the land for a speedway.

Leon Johnson's family-owned property in the area. Johnson's father, Ted Johnson, was a local minister and did not want the speedway in their neighborhood.

"We had dirt tracks in the area. They might have had 200 people," Leon Johnson said.

His father felt there was "a lot of debauchery" in racing so he started a petition, gathering signatures of people opposing the project.

Johnson said he remembers Moore and Carrier visiting his home and informing them that due to community opposition, they were changing their plans for the speedway. As a result, they purchased land in Bristol, rather than moving forward with plans for a raceway in Piney Flats.

"We heard that some people were against it, so we had a meeting to listen to what the community had to say," Moore, who died in 2021, told local racing historian David McGee. "Most everybody there was for us, but there were two preachers who didn't like it. They thought racing would bring in all kinds of undesirable elements -- drinking and gambling and wild women--so we decided not to go."

Instead, they found a 100-acre farm a few miles northeast of Highway 11E closer to Bristol and Winnie Moore Carter was ready to sell.

Bristol Motor Speedway was then constructed.

Mark Carrier, Larry Carrier's son, noted that his father never sold alcohol at the track, which was an issue that churches in Piney Flats had been concerned about.

Johnson said he remembered eventually attending the races at Bristol, and always wondered what would have happened if the Piney Flats plans moved forward. He recalled that it cost $6 to see a race.

Each spring and fall, Piney Flats benefits from race fans heading to Bristol Motor Speedway. "Welcome Race Fans" banners can be seen in front of every gas station and restaurant. Signs greet passing cars, welcoming them to do business in Piney Flats.

Today, Bristol Motor Speedway is one of the world's largest stadiums, and once marked an incredible 54 consecutive sellouts. It continues to attract fans from all 50 states and more than a dozen foreign countries.

This gentleman came into Piney Flats on his motorcycle in 1914. He's pictured here along Main Street in the village. (Courtesy Piney Flats Historical Society)

CHAPTER EIGHT

Historic Preservation

Jim Hager and his wife, Mary Ann Hager, a longtime president of the Piney Flats Historical Society, bought an historic family home at the corner of Main Street and Piney Flats Road in the center of the village in 1999. The couple had lived in Ohio for many years but decided to retire in Piney Flats, Mary Ann's family's native home. They purchased the Hughes home, which is named after its original owner, and was built before the Civil War. It's a two-story Queen Anne style residence with whiteboard siding.

The couple attempted to keep as much historic character as possible, Mary Ann Hager said. They kept the original woodwork, plaster walls, and wavy glass windows. They did give the home some modern conveniences, such as three bathrooms and air conditioning.

The Hughes House features many Queen Anne-style features, including intricate woodworking. (Photo by author)

Previous owners included Samuel R. Wolfe and his wife Tommie, and A.C. and Nell Hughes Campbell, according to deed records.

Since purchasing and restoring their home, the Hagers began to discover changes in the community. At least two historic homes nearby fell into disrepair and were demolished.

"At that point, I thought, which house was next," Mary Ann Hager said.

The couple and others in the neighborhood were also concerned about new residential, commercial, and industrial development in Piney Flats that threatened the village.

The couple contacted the county planning staff who suggested historic district status.

The Hagers then got busy, the Bristol Herald Courier said.

First, they put together a list of buildings that played part in the village's history. The list of 17 structures included 14 homes, the Wolfe Brothers

142

Take a look at this view from the front porch of the Hughes House. The neighbor's beautiful brick residence can be seen next door in the distance. (Photo by author)

factory, the Mitchell Carr General Store, and the Piney Flats United Methodist Church. They then conducted quite a bit of research and wrote guidelines for the new historic district.

Then came the hard part. They had to convince their neighbors to approve and join the district. Most neighbors eventually approved the plans;

about 90 percent of the community signed the petition seeking the historic zoning designation.

In 2009, the Sullivan County Commission unanimously approved plans to create the Piney Flats Village, the county's second historic district. The decision essentially protected the village's historic character for generations to come. The designation means some construction projects have to be approved by the Sullivan County Historic Zoning Commission, which also must approve similar projects in the Blountville Historic District, the nearby community that serves as the county seat.

The historic zoning district provides a sense of pride for the community and increases property values.

The Piney Flats Historical Society organized and became a 501c3 non-profit. It meets often to discuss history, preservation, and community events. They have developed plaques that property owners can put on their homes and outbuildings describing each structure's significance. The organization also publishes a newsletter and calendars highlighting the neighborhood's history and residents.

The Hal Maasengill House, also known as the Simerly House, features a handsome sign out front. (Photo by author)

144

Hager said the group's success with Sullivan County motivated them to turn their attention toward earning a place on the National Register of Historic Places.

"We invited the Tennessee Historical Commission to come visit our village and see if we were eligible for the National Register," she told the Johnson City Press. "We had a lovely reception here in the little village for four members of the THC and they said, 'yes, go for it.' We started working on that in early 2010, working on our National Register designation."

That designation came a year later as the Piney Flats Village was placed on the National Register in November of 2011.

Three years later, the state of Tennessee further recognized the village by placing a historical marker in the commercial district along U.S. Highway 11E at Piney Flats Road.

Whether through its architecture, culture, or history, Hager said she was happy that the marker would help educate passersby on Piney Flats Village. Two large welcome signs also sit at the two ends of Main Street, welcoming visitors to the village. The historical society maintains and decorates the signs.

The need for preservation continues in 2022.

The Wolfe Brothers factory, once the heart and soul of Piney Flats, saw its demise. The property became a liability problem and required demolition. As some locals would say, one strong gust of wind could have blown the building down.

Locals were able to salvage some items from the building. Items and materials went to the nearby Rocky Mount Historic Site, where some were sold to the public; others went to local archives and residents. The historical society assisted in developing an historic kiosk at the site so locals and visitors would continue to learn about the factory and its importance in Piney Flats history.

The Hughes House is covered in snow in this wintry scene. For many years, the community has decorated a Christmas tree near the home. (Courtesy Piney Flats Historical Society)

CHAPTER NINE

Miscellaneous History

Horse Show

The Piney Flats Horse Show was held annually beginning in 1962 at the E.L. "Ned" King Farm in Piney Flats. It was a two-day event sponsored by the Piney Flats Ruritan Club through its partnership with local, state, and national walking horse associations. Owners and their horses from many surrounding states attended the event. Hundreds of spectators also attended each summer.

A large horse show was once held in Piney Flats. (Courtesy Janie Torbett)

The event was held at King's farm, a large property between Austin Springs Road and U.S. Highway 11E, south of Mary Hughes School. King, who died in 1990 at the age of 90, and is pictured on his horse on this page, managed the event. The popular show had dozens of events and featured participants of all ages, including a three-year-old child in 1968. The Ruritan Club used proceeds from the event to fund various community projects.

Sullivan County Fair

During the first half of the 20th century, a large community fair was held in Piney Flats. The annual Sullivan County Fair was held at Locust Grove School in the Pickens Bridge Road area from 1909 until 1931. Active community leaders who organized the fairs included M.D. Massengill, E.A. Torbett, Jim Snapp, J.N. Arrants, J.B. Wolfe, John and Richard Anderson, and W.A. Hughes. In 1932 the fair was moved to the Mary Hughes School.

"The Sullivan County Fair is for all the people of Sullivan County," according to an article in the Bristol Herald Courier. "This fair belongs to every farm home in the county. We want the fair to stimulate not only increased production but also improvement of quality in farm products."

The fair included educational exhibits, farm implements, machinery of all kinds, household conveniences, musical instruments, special articles of merchandise, automobiles, charts and posters, and other items of real educational value. The fair also invited local experts to give demonstrations.

In 1922, Piney Flats became the primary site of the Sullivan County Fair--the fair for several years was held in various locations around the county--and many prizes and ribbons were given out. The newspaper reported that prizes were awarded to the ugliest man on the grounds and one to the largest family. A prize was also given to the man who could take off a Ford tire and replace it in the shortest time.

In 1932, the Sullivan County Fair moved from nearby Locust Grove to Mary Hughes School, where it continued to be held annually for several years. One year, more than 6,000 people attended the fair. Unfortunately, the fair eventually became so large that it could no longer be accommodated in Piney Flats, and it was moved to Blountville in the late 1930s.

Volunteer Fire Department

The community of Piney Flats was growing in the mid-20th century and residents needed a fire department. On Oct. 23, 1955, a group of citizens sponsored by the Piney Flats Ruritan Club, which consisted of local farmers

The early Piney Flats Volunteer Fire Department is pictured here. It was established in the 1950s. (Courtesy Janie Torbett)

and businessmen, met in the auditorium of Mary Hughes School to organize and form a new fire department.

Earl Trivett became the department's first fire chief, and George Cross was named president. They obtained a long list of phone numbers of individuals in the community who were ready to volunteer their time to provide fire protection for Piney Flats. The first firemen included Wayne Hamilton, Jimmie D. Hicks, Haskel Webb, Kyle McKinney, Creed Starnes, Bennie Young, Tom Persinger, Sam Sanders, Glen Elsea, Cecil Martin, Jerry Ramsey, Howard Lyle Torbett, Joe Hughes, Gene Torbett and Cross, the president, according to news reports.

Piney Flats Volunteer Fire Department Station 2 is located on Rocky Springs Road near its intersection with Alison Road. (Photo by author)

Soon after, the department acquired a $1,500 1939 Diamond-T fire truck from Reisterston, Maryland. The truck, which had a 200-gallon tank and could deliver more than 500 gallons of water per minute, was stored in a small garage building next to Mr. Trivett's service station at the Piney Flats crossroads.

Since the beginning, the department has cooperated with other volunteer fire departments in Sullivan County, including those in nearby Bluff City and Blountville. With the assistance of the Ruritan Club, the department added more equipment. Two years after its formation, the department built a new station and purchased an 1800-gallon water tank truck.

In late 1978, the city of Elizabethton, Carter County, and Sullivan County granted the fire department land at the Tri-County Industrial Park for a new station. The municipalities sold the department the land for $1, according to a deed.

Another station was constructed in the late 1980s on Rocky Springs Road near its intersection with Allison Road. At first, the station housed an engine and a tanker.

Piney Flats Ruritan Club

The Piney Flats Ruritan Club, the first in Sullivan County, was established in 1954. Ted Johnson was named the first president, according to an article in the Johnson City Press. Other officers included Wilbur Smalling, John D. Smalling, J.B. Snapp Jr., Joe Hughes, Ivan Malone, and John Martin. At first, the club met at Mary Hughes School, but later developed a community center in 1969. The Ruritan Club has sponsored horse shows, Piney Flats Days, beauty pageants, and other events.

Many successful local residents have joined the Piney Flats Ruritan Club over the years. In early 1959, Country music artist Tennessee Ernie Ford accepted an honorary membership to join the club. Ford was a Sullivan County native and mentioned Piney Flats on his national television show. The noted actor accepted the membership by letter from his California residence, according to the Bristol Herald Courier. Ford, who grew up in nearby Bristol, had family that lived in Piney Flats.

Tennessee Ernie Ford, the famed Bristol musician, had several family connections to Piney Flats. He joined the Ruritan Club as an honorary member. This photo was distributed to media for his television show.

Tri-County Industrial Park

Thousands of people clock in to work daily at the Tri-County Industrial Park in Piney Flats. It's located on the north side of the historic district and covers more than 1,000 acres.

Since World War II, the industrial park concept has come to characterize the grouped setting of industrial activity within urbanized areas. In most cases, the property includes installed utilities, highly accessible highways, and rail connections to the sites. Acceptance of the industrial park concept has grown rapidly over the years; many communities began developing parks in the 1960s and 1970s.

In that period, Sullivan County and its surrounding communities felt there was a need to increase job creation in the Northeast Tennessee region. In order to compete for manufacturing facilities throughout the southeastern U.S., planning began on the establishment of a regional industrial park. The park was developed in the early 1970's by four communities, including Sullivan County, the city of Johnson City, the city of Elizabethton and Carter County. The partnership grew out of necessity for a regional park to attract large industries, and the need for grant funding to make it successful. Both were important factors in the communities coming together for the success of the park.

Originally, there were seven tracts of land included in the project, including several farms. The seven original tracts totaled 780 acres of land. Based on land values at the time, land acquisition costs were $1 million for the 780 acres. The Appalachian Regional Commission granted funding for the project.

Industry has always been important in Piney Flats. Early businesses in Piney Flats included a blacksmith, a livery stable, machine shops, a canning factory, a feather-packing operation, and a hoop factory, which manufactured barrels of wood and hoops from tree bark. There were also several general stores.

Two businesses sold farm machinery and fertilizer: J.E. Smalling and Eli Anderson and Son. James White operated a tanning yard near Rocky

Springs. Oliver's Distillery was located in Weavers Branch and produced brandy before World War I. Local farmers maintained large orchards and supplied apple cider to the distillery. Several residents made apple butter from the local orchards.

Piney Flats First Baptist Church

A Southern Baptist Church had long been sought in the community when the Piney Flats First Baptist Church was first established in the late 1950s. The vision of resident Earl Anderson, a meeting was first held in 1959 at Mary Hughes School to establish a Baptist church.

The first congregants came from Rocky Springs Union Church, Piney Flats Union Church, First Baptist Church of Bluff City, and others. Property was originally purchased and donated along U.S. Highway 11E. The congregation built a one-story brick structure, where the first church meeting was held June 17, 1959.

Additional property has been purchased over the years, including in 1964, when the congregation constructed a parsonage. The church's first expansion was reported in 1969 and the second addition was completed in 1987, according to a church history. Eventually, a nearby grocery store building and more property were purchased to serve as an activities building for the church.

The congregation has continued to grow, and a new sanctuary began construction in 2003. An additional multi-purpose facility was constructed in 2013.

Mary Hughes is pictured with a World War I military service flag. Mary Hughes School's football team is below. (Photos courtesy Piney Flats Historical Society)

Bibliography

Big Stone Gap Post. Various articles on Daniel Boone tree.

Bristol Herald Courier. Various articles on Piney Flats, 1940 – 2012.

Grant, Meredith Anne, "Internal Dissent: East Tennessee's Civil War, 1849-1865." (2008). Electronic Theses and Dissertations. Paper 1962. https://dc.etsu.edu/etd/1962

Johnson City Press. Various articles on Piney Flats.

Holston Territory Genealogical Society. "Families and History of Sullivan County, Tennessee Volume 1 1772-1992." Waynesville, N.C.: Walsworth Publishing, 1992.

Morrell, Gene. "Mountain Memories." Blountville, Tenn.: Sullivan County News, 1977-1979.

New Bethel Presbyterian Church. "The New Bethel Bicentennial 1782-1982." Johnson City, Tenn.: The Overmountain Press, 1982.

Piney Flats First Baptist Church. "History." https://www.pineyflatsbaptist.org/history.

Piney Flats Historical Society. "Piney Flats Village Voice." 2008-2010.

Rocky Mount State Historic Site. "Our History." http://www.rockymountmuseum.com.

Sullivan County. "Piney Flats Village Historic District Design Guidelines." 2009.

Sullivan County News. Various articles on Piney Flats.

Taylor, Oliver. "Sullivan County: Sullivan County, Tennessee." Johnson City, Tenn.: The Overmountain Press, 1988.

Tennessee Valley Authority. "The Upper Holston Projects, Technical Report No. 14, Watauga, South Holston, Boone, and Fort Patrick Henry." Washington, D.C.: U. S. Government Printing Office, 1958.

U.S. Department of Interior. "Boone Hydroelectric Project." National Register of Historic Places, 2017.
--"Devault-Masengill House." National Register of Historic Places nomination form, 1985.
--"Finlay Alison House." National Register of Historic Places nomination form, 1973.
--"Piney Flats Historic District." National Register of Historic Places nomination form, 2011.
--"Rocky Mount." National Register of Historic Places nomination form, 1970.